THE PROPERTY L
The Hidden Reality b
Housing Crisi

Bob Colenutt

First published in Great Britain in 2020 by

Policy Press
University of Bristol
1-9 Old Park Hill
Bristol
BS2 8BB
UK
t: +44 (0)117 954 5940
pp-info@bristol.ac.uk
www.policypress.co.uk

North America office:
Policy Press
c/o The University of Chicago Press
1427 East 60th Street
Chicago, IL 60637, USA
t: +1 773 702 7700
f: +1 773-702-9756
sales@press.uchicago.edu
www.press.uchicago.edu

British Library Cataloguing in Publication Data
A catalogue record for this book is available from the British Library

Library of Congress Cataloging-in-Publication Data
A catalog record for this book has been requested

ISBN 978-1-4473-4049-2 (hardcover)
ISBN 978-1-4473-4816-0 (paperback)
ISBN 978-1-4473-5024-8 (ePub)
ISBN 978-1-4473-5023-1 (ePdf)

Cover design by Andrew Corbett
Front cover image: Schankz/Bigstock

What concerns me is less the mechanics of the transition than the power and ideological roadblocks that have so far prevented any of them from taking place on anything close to the scale required.

Naomi Klein, This changes everything, 2014

Contents

Acknowledgements

This book is dedicated to Ted Bowman, who chaired the North Southwark Community Development Group (NSCDG) in South London from 1972 until his death in 2014. He was an extraordinary community activist and mentor, without whom this book would not have been written. His story and its pivotal role in the book is explained in the Preface.

Many others have been my friends and comrades, past and present, on my journey. They include George Nicholson, Iain Tuckett, Geoff Williams, Theresa McDonagh, Pete McDonagh, Hilary Wainwright, Stefan de Corte, Connie Hunt, Fred Robinson, Andy Clarke, David Harvey, Bill Bunge, Michael Edwards, Allan Cochrane, Rudy Daley, Nick Kochan, Jeremy Grint, Jerry Flynn, Tim Marshall, Matt Scott, Sue Brownill, Martin Field, Chris Durkin, Sabine Coady Schaebitz, the Highbury Housing Group and many more, all of whom have been hugely influential and have guided and challenged my thinking and politics in many ways.

Deborah and my family have been a rock and amazing advisors, supporters and critics throughout the writing of this book and for many years beforehand. I also want to thank Steve Butterworth for his excellent online Housing and Planning Update, which has kept me on the ball on all matters housing (and Northamptonshire). I must also thank all those who kindly gave their time to be interviewed for this book. Finally, I must not forget Bristol University Press, who gave me a contract and published this book.

Bob Colenutt
Oxford
2020

Preface

Ted is a print worker. He lives with his family in a rented flat in a Church Commissioners block in North Southwark, South London, close to the River Thames. His wife, Hilda, works in a local school. They have lived in the area all their lives. Ted chairs a community group worried about plans by the council to zone the area for 'City and West End Uses'. Some students came into the community centre to offer to help. I was one of those students. That was 47 years ago.

I stayed in North Southwark working as a community planner with Ted and my colleague George. I later moved on when our grant funding was cut off to work for the Joint Docklands Action Group, in London Docklands. My journey took me into local government via a spell in the Docklands Unit at the Greater London Council (GLC) in its final years before the abolition of the GLC by the Thatcher government. I worked for local councils elsewhere in London, first, as a local councillor, then as a regeneration officer trying to make a difference from inside local government. Ted and his community group, the North Southwark Community Development Group, kept going.

'City and West End Uses' did come into North Southwark – with a vengeance. Flats in Ted's block were progressively sold off at West End prices to young professionals as elderly residents passed away or moved out. The area was transformed beyond recognition. All down the river, from Waterloo Bridge to Tower Bridge and then into the Docklands, land values rocketed through the 1980s and 1990s. Luxury flats, office blocks and restaurants were crammed onto the riverfront. The housing needs of local people took second place. Big money poured in as the government backed the developers time and time again. The property market triumphed. Most of the local councils caved in to pressure and some council leaders happily sat on government development boards such as the London Docklands Development Corporation; several senior planning officers went through a revolving door to work for the developers.

Ted was at the helm of his group through it all for 40 years. He died in 2014. There were small concessions to the community, and some important victories when councils put up a fight. Coin Street Community Builders housing scheme at Waterloo was the biggest victory. However, elsewhere, the needs of the community for decent housing and environment, and the protection of local shops and services, were in full-scale retreat. The voices of ordinary people and their needs were overwhelmed.

Downstream, the Docklands were put to the sword by the government and the developers: the docks were sold off; local plans were scrapped; and the property market took over. The building of Canary Wharf was underwritten by gigantic government tax breaks, and acres of luxury flats were built along the river, reaching deep into the Royal Docks. The final indignity was giving permission for London City Airport, now generating a procession of jets screaming over houses and flats of Custom House communities a few hundred feet below.

In the battle for land in London Docklands in 1985, Pat Hanshaw, chair of the Association of Wapping Organisations, put it this way:

> There has been a lot of talk about land; the ownership of land; land for this, land for that. But Docklands is not about land. It's about people and the birthright of the people is being sold off. Although the people have never owned the land they have lived on it, worked on it, and died on it. It is their heritage. It should be their future. ('Our future in Docklands' poster, Docklands Poster Project, 1985)

Seventy miles to the north of London is the county of Northamptonshire. I worked there as a local government planning officer, and later as a planning researcher at the University of Northampton, where I became aware of another dimension of the hidden reality behind the housing crisis. This time, it was not the commercial developers and their stranglehold on housing development and local government in London, but the enormous power of landowners and the volume housebuilders – the Barratts, Wimpeys and Persimmons of this world – who have a similar grip on the provision of new housing in that county, and in many other counties, that lie in the far-flung commuter belt outside London. Here, as in London, the property market – landowners, financiers, developers and their agents – exercise huge influence over the pattern of growth in the county and wider region, often with the full backing of the central government.

It is not just in the South East of England where landowners and developers have so much of their own way. It is the same in many villages, towns and cities in the North and Midlands – in fact, all across the UK. Here too, local communities are faced with unaffordable house prices and a lack of new social housing. The volume builders replicate their layouts, designs and pricing mechanisms from Land's End to John o' Groats. The town and country planning system appears to be quite powerless to make a difference; if anything, it seems to help the development machine on its way. There are alternative housebuilders such as housing associations and community land trusts but they are not enough – and many are themselves getting tangled up with financial institutions and the property market.

Each time local people are told 'don't worry, new developments are going to be quite small and user-friendly and, anyway, there will be affordable houses and community services such as health centres and new bus routes as a spin-off from development'. The plans look impressive but it never seems to end that way. Developments are bigger than expected. The services never arrive or get there years after they are promised. Affordable housing gets squeezed; the word 'affordable' is redefined by the government and the housebuilders so that it is not actually affordable for many. The voice of local communities is relegated to the sidelines. The crumbs from the property table seem to get small and smaller. The developers focus relentlessly on land and its value, not the people who live on it; more often than not, local authorities join in.

Ted's story is the starting point of this book about what lies behind the housing crisis – and what it would take to stop the property machine in its tracks and allow housing and community needs to finally be met. My mission is to explain the economic and political forces which ensure that local communities are powerless to stop the lack of affordability and the rise in homelessness in their neighbourhoods. As we shall see, part of the problem is that the town planning system, which was originally intended to be the servant of the people, has now become the servant of the landowner and development industry.

We have reached the point where many planners will not speak openly about how the property market is manipulating the town planning system – that suits the property industry and its powerful lobby very nicely. The real purpose of planning and housing policy should be to regulate the property market and offer alternatives so that all communities can truly benefit. We are miles away from that at the moment. However, unless we get there soon, the housing crisis is set to continue indefinitely.

An overview of the book

This book is primarily about the housing crisis in England, although, of course, there is a housing crisis in Scotland, Wales and Northern Ireland with similar land, property market and government forces at work. However, from the point of view of investment in property, the English property market is the heartland of power in land and property in the UK – and within England, most investment interest and value in land and property is in selected areas of London and the South East of England. The geography of this property power not only impacts on those southern locations and communities; it also ripples out across the UK, and exercises extraordinary influence over the politics and economy of the UK as a whole. London and the South East is also the area of the country in which the author has lived and worked for many years and can therefore draw on his own experience of community development and local planning.

Chapter 1 introduces the themes of the book. It highlights the main blockages to solving the UK's permanent housing crisis, focusing on the emergence of the finance–housebuilding complex and its close relationship to government.

In Chapter 2, we examine the housing shortages that underlie the housing crisis. What do we mean by shortages? How have these been twisted into a numbers game that is played by the government and housebuilders to confuse and often mislead the public?

Chapter 3 focuses on the business model of the housebuilders, in particular, the politics of the business model. What are the key business factors, such as profits and land value, for which developers and landowners seek support, and usually get it, from the government?

Chapter 4 looks at the bigger picture of the overburdening presence of property and housing finance in the UK economy. This is a critical context for understanding the role of the government in creating its own barriers to resolving the housing crisis.

Chapter 5 turns to the property lobby: the lobby groups that have extraordinary political access to the highest levels of government. These lobbies have also created an environment where their technical and professional knowledge has become the first port of call for the government and civil servants; as such, they are as a major obstacle to change.

Chapter 6 examines three examples of how the property lobby has influenced national policy on planning and housing, and, in doing so, has prolonged the housing crisis. The first example is the ill-fated Growth Areas programme in the Sustainable Communities Plan of New Labour in the 2000s; the second is how the property lobby directly influenced the writing of the *National Planning Policy Framework* (NPPF) (DCLG, 2012) of the Coalition government in 2012; and the third example is the manipulation by the property lobby of the viability assessment process for planning obligations, which has directly reduced the amount of affordable housing provided by developers. This measure was introduced by the government after the financial crash and written into the NPPF – and it continues to dominate the provision of affordable housing to this day.

Chapter 7 is about the impact of the 2008 financial crash and its continuing aftermath on the scale of the housing crisis. The political and economic fallout from 2008 continues to act as a major block to the radical reform of housing and town planning policy.

Chapter 8 looks at the housebuilding companies and their strategies for avoiding building social and truly affordable housing.

Chapter 9 focuses on the social and affordable housing sector and how this has increasingly become swallowed up by the finance–housebuilding complex, creating a further barrier to change.

Chapter 10 introduces two local case studies– one from Oxford and the other from London – of the influence of the finance–housebuilding complex reaching down to the level of day-to-day planning decisions made by local authorities, making planning for local communities a huge struggle that local authorities and communities often end up losing.

Chapter 11, the final chapter, calls for a decisive break from the policies and practices that have strangled social and affordable housing development over the past 40 years.

A Postscript follows which comments on the implications of Brexit and the 2019 General Election result for housing, communities and the power of the property lobby.

1

The finance–housebuilding complex

Over decades, the UK housing crisis has persisted despite dozens of studies, government statements and community protests. Governments of all colours have announced new policies and interventions but nothing fundamental has changed. Despite intense campaigning by housing charities, and constituents queuing at the surgeries of Members of Parliament (MPs), there is an apparently unending housing shortage and a shocking lack of affordable and social homes. Experts tell us that we are short of 4 million homes, that thousands are homeless, that 1.2 million are on council waiting lists and that 'one million private tenants are in deep poverty' (Doward, 2018), but no effective action is taken. The housing crisis gets worse even as the number of think-tank reports, special commissions and select committees increases. Why is the housing system so impervious to change? What are the roadblocks?

In 1961, President Eisenhower talked of a 'military–industrial complex' to explain the power and interlocking nature of industry, finance and government in the military-related sectors of the economy. This book argues that at the root of the housing crisis, there is a 'finance–housebuilding complex' in the land and property market in the UK. It consists of close links between financial institutions, the government, political parties, landowners and developers. Increasingly, local authorities and housing associations are being drawn in. Government and the housebuilding industry have become interdependent. For both, they are mutually indispensable. This fatal embrace is the hidden reality behind the housing crisis.

The finance–housebuilding complex has immense power and patronage, which has grown remorselessly over the last 30 years. It is the major blockage to change. Yet, its composition, assumptions, working practices, lobbying and impact are largely unexamined and hidden from public scrutiny. By putting the finance–housebuilding complex and its lobbying power under the microscope, it is possible to reveal how reforms that would help to tackle the housing crisis have been blocked time and again – with the collusion of HM Treasury.

To understand the real challenge of the housing crisis, it is essential to examine the lobbyists, pressure groups and political forces inside and outside Whitehall that make up this complex of power. Equally importantly, we need to take a close look at the key policy issues on which it lobbies, and why the government has been so amenable to this lobby. For that, we must examine the business models of the land and property industries and the investor calculations that drive housing development decisions. We must also look closely at government policy on housing and land and how they interact with the property industry.

The book will describe how the national housebuilding sector operates and how its business practices have evolved. It will explain how this sector and its backers in finance, rather than helping to solve the housing crisis, are creating housing shortages and a lack of affordability, at the same time as generating huge profits for investors, landowners and housebuilders. Of course, many homeowners have benefitted from price rises too, and this divide and rule is of immense value to the property lobby.

In boom or slump, landowners and volume housebuilders do not build enough housing to meet the demand for homes. Furthermore, despite their public promises and reassurances, they show remarkably little flexibility in the way in which they respond to criticism. Their well-orchestrated lobbies identify shortcomings in everyone else, for example, the town planning system, local authorities, Nimbys or government regulation. Never do they look at themselves and ask what responsibility they have for the housing crisis. In fact, in many ways, they do not see it as their concern – and perhaps they are right: they build houses and make profits from land; they are not charities or public bodies. Unless the government tells them that they must do things differently, they will carry on as before. So, why have successive governments been so timid and unwilling to do so?

The scale of the crisis

It is not as if the government and Whitehall are not fully aware of the facts of the housing crisis. Its own civil servants have produced dozens of reports and statistics that spell out the scale of the crisis. Housing experts in universities, think tanks and housing agencies monitor in detail the facts of affordability, land prices, homelessness and the shortages of new supply. Shelter and the Joseph Rowntree Foundation have been describing the social impact on families and communities for decades. Also, over decades, regular visits by experts and politicians to European countries like the Netherlands and Sweden, where they do planning and housing much better, have made no impact on UK housing and planning whatsoever. Almost every week, another shock report or official statement comes out, but after a day or so, we are back to where we were.

One such report was published by the Resolution Foundation in 2018, showing that a third of young people born in the 1980s and 1990s will never own their own home (Resolution Foundation, 2018). There was a moment of shock at the implications of this study but no action followed. Even the government admitted that the housing market was 'broken' – an apparently dramatic confession. Yet, their response was so weak as to barely register in the public consciousness a few weeks later. There was the usual rapid rotation of housing ministers so that everyone lost track of who was responsible. Government announcements were made in response to the crisis but they seemed to consist of political spin, or ineffective tinkering. Why is this? Who or what is holding the government back, not just the current government, but many before, from taking necessary action?

Communities all over the country, local councillors and MPs know only too well the length of housing waiting lists, the desperation of homeless families and the sky-high private sector rents. They also experience the daily pressures of responding to developers and landowners wanting to pack more development onto sites, seeking to bend the rules of planning regulation and control. These pressures, justified in terms of investment or growth, get stronger and stronger over the years. It has not just crept up on us, but accelerated since the 1980s, taking a sharper turn since the recession and the onset of austerity after 2008. Since then, it has continued all through the housing boom years of 2012–18.

Local authorities were told by the government from the 1980s onwards that there was less money for them to build housing for those in need. They must depend on the volume housebuilders to build new stock and renovate run-down estates, and try to negotiate a paltry amount of affordable housing as 'planning gain'. Furthermore, as these same volume builders annually buy hundreds of hectares of additional long-term development land on a speculative basis, building land is wildly expensive, such that local authorities (and community housing groups) are unable to intervene in the land market themselves – and if they do, spiralling land prices make new housing unaffordable.

A further squeeze on land and affordability has come from the increase in overseas investment in property noted across many cities around the world. Floods of money into luxury property have ratcheted up the power of the property sector in the UK, giving it extraordinary leverage with politicians, the government and local decision-makers. London property is an especially attractive location for overseas investors and wealth funds. Kollewe reported that in 2014 London was by far the favoured global location for 'Ultra High Net Worth Individuals', defined as individuals with fortunes of over £30 million (Kollewe, 2014). More recently encouraged by the fall in the pound against other currencies due to Brexit, London property is now considered a 'bargain' for overseas investors, according to property agents Knight Frank. Tell that to ordinary folk wanting to buy or rent in London.

Market dependency

The combination of public austerity and the private property boom has added a new twist to the ideological battle over land and property. There has always been ideology in abundance in housing: free markets versus government spending and intervention; homeownership versus social renting; housing growth versus green belts. However, reliance on market growth by successive governments, allowing property market power and property investment to ratchet ever upwards, is without doubt a more powerful ideology. Owen Jones (2014: 253) argues in his book *The establishment* that the New Labour governments of the 2000s made a Faustian pact with the City, saying 'Don't kill the goose that lays the golden egg', in other words, public services can be funded from City financial services. However, at root, that goose is invariably the property investment market – and this has consequences.

It was because of this default market dependency that New Labour governments in 1997–2010, even with large parliamentary majorities, made only minor interventions in the land and property markets. The Right to Buy council housing policy, begun by the Thatcher government in 1980, relentlessly continued to reduce the social housing stock throughout the 1990s and 2000s. Relatively few new social homes were built. The affordability of new market housing continued to decline, and reliance on the volume housebuilders increased. The finance–housebuilding complex sailed on.

New Labour, increasingly anxious about shortages of both market and affordable housing, commissioned expert investigations, such as the Barker (2004) report on housing supply, and launched ambitious plans, notably the Sustainable Communities Plan in 2003. However, as Chapter 6 explains, there was a fatal flaw in the New Labour analysis: it relied on a rising property market to deliver a boost to new market housing with the promise of new affordable housing and the refurbishment of council estates funded off the back of this growth. It misguidedly believed that because of the booming property market of the early 2000s, the government could step back from direct delivery and could rely upon the private sector to meet the government's ambitious housing targets. There was no need to go back to the bad old days of funding and building new council housing.

The housebuilding companies and the landowners happily agreed to the new pact with the government. They welcomed the privileged status that they were given and snapped up the land that was made available through the planning system, not to mention the financial stimulus that was also offered. What the government forgot, or chose to ignore, was that if you make new housing and planning 'growth dependent', the price, tenure and location of new housing will depend on market forces and fluctuations – and new building will grind to a halt when the market crashes (Rydin, 2013).

To make matters worse, it became obvious that the raft of measures relating to the quality of new housing development, such as affordable housing, community facilities, low carbon construction, local public transport initiatives and high-quality designs, were also dependent on cross-subsidies from the profits of the housing market. Thus, when the crash came in 2008, the sustainable development agenda that was a prominent feature of the 2000–07 period wound down very rapidly. As an underlying principle of new development, sustainability was quickly de-prioritised (in spite of the glaring facts of climate change) by successive governments in the austerity years that followed. Furthermore, even as the country emerged from the recession, the finance–housebuilding complex was able to convince the government (it was not difficult) that sustainability measures were burdens that would reduce their margins in a fragile economic environment, and therefore threaten the achievement of government housing targets.

The lack of a coherent or emphatic government response to the national housing crisis is partly due to the fact that its political impact varies across the country. There is a specific regional politics of housing in high market demand parts of the country in the South East, where there are high prices, intense development pressures and an acute awareness of the politics of planning and housing in local government. In lower demand areas, such as parts of the North-East, the North-West and Central Lancashire towns, for example, the politics and economics are different. Although there are severe housing deficiencies, there is less pressure for market-led development; indeed, local authorities often seek out developers and offer them incentives to build. In such areas, it is more difficult to see the development industry as out of control and needing radical reform.

Yet, the housing investment and housebuilding market is a national market. Housebuilders hold a national portfolio of land and planning permissions. This is sometimes difficult to see when London and the South East are more profitable investment locations than 'the North'. Moreover, the difference between 'high demand' areas and 'low demand' areas should not be exaggerated to justify taking no national policy action, nor should it be used to hide the level of housing deprivation in every city, town and village in the country, whether north or south. Although regional contrasts make a coherent national policy response complicated, the housing crisis is a national disgrace and requires a national response.

Scapegoating planning

Conveniently for both Conservative and Labour governments, the profession of town planning, a relatively small and struggling regulatory part of local government, was outrageously scapegoated by politicians (and some academics) as being a principal cause of the shortage of new homes. The government, and the property lobby, had a catalogue of complaints. They claimed that planners were not allocating enough land for housing, or were stopping new building by withholding planning consents, or were too slow, or were imposing unreasonable obligations and conditions on developers. The Town and Country Planning Association (TCPA) and the Royal Town Planning Institute (RTPI) fought back, saying that the planners were just doing their job scrutinising planning applications thoroughly and following the law in preparing plans and consulting the public.

There is also no doubt that these attacks put the planners on the defensive. It is true that mistakes had been made over the design of high-rise blocks, and local people were often not properly consulted over planning or housing schemes. Alice Coleman wrote a book in 1985 that went as far as claiming that social breakdown in the UK was caused by the poor design of public housing estates (Coleman, 1985). In the US, Jane Jacobs (1961) famously attacked planners and road builders for wrecking viable neighbourhoods in New York. Much the same happened in the UK in the battle for land and community in London (Ambrose and Colenutt, 1975; Wates, 1976). Community groups found that town planning, rather than protecting communities, made local conditions worse by opening the doors to property speculation and gentrification.

At that time, very few looked at what was happening to the housing supply market, where the volume housebuilders operated. Michael Ball's (1983) path-breaking book on speculative housebuilding and the planning system was a major exception. How did the housebuilding market work? Why was the planning system so ineffective? Why was there a shortage of new housing? For the first time, there was a focus on landowners, housebuilders and their business models.

Throughout the angry exchange of accusations and allegations about who was to blame for the housing crisis, whether planners or developers, local authorities or landowners, the finance–housebuilding complex steadily accumulated more power and political influence throughout the 1980s, 1990s and 2000s. It was only during the financial crash of 2008 that the finger of blame for the collapse in the property market was placed, for a moment, on greedy developers and sub-prime mortgages, though after a few rocky months, the key companies in the finance–housebuilding complex came through largely unscathed. After this regrouping, these companies and their allies in Parliament continued their attack on planners and local authorities for the shortage of new housing.

Community action

Frustrated by the lack of action on housing by the government and property sector, many communities have decided to do their own housebuilding, setting up community land trusts, development trusts, self-build groups and housing cooperatives to build housing at sensible rents and prices. However, they are up against it. Land prices, construction costs and professional fees are all massive barriers to voluntary groups.

Thus, community-led housing initiatives typically have a multi-year struggle to achieve even a tiny provision of affordable housing. The iconic Coin Street Community Builders (CSCB) on London's South Bank began their campaign in 1974. Now, 45 years on, they have completed 250 low-rent cooperatively run flats and houses with gardens plus workshops and open space on 13 acres – quite an achievement in the centre of London. None of this would have happened without support from the Greater London Council (GLC), who passed the Coin Street sites over to CSCB for a token sum hours before the GLC was abolished. Since then, it has taken decades of single-minded community determination to assemble land, finance and the right to build high-quality low-rent homes on the Thames riverfront.[1]

Compare this with another iconic development epitomising almost the opposite set of social and economic values just down the road at Canary Wharf in London Docklands. With high-level government intervention in the form of £6 billion of government tax breaks, land assembly and transport investment, 1.5 million square metres of office space have been built in the space of 20 years. Also, compare Coin Street with the 10,000 housing units that are to be built mainly for sale on the Greenwich Peninsula. This scheme is being built on land reclaimed with public money that was then sold for a song to a Hong Kong property company. The public subsidy for this deal alone is vastly more than the annual government subsidy for all community-led housing schemes across the whole of London.

The lesson that many draw from community-led housing projects across the country is that the planning system, contrary to the accusations of the property lobby, encourages and facilitates the private housebuilding sector and commercial developers, while community-led schemes face scepticism and bureaucratic obstruction (Field, 2020). The big picture is that under these conditions, the community-led housing sector poses no threat to the finance–housebuilding complex – and that is the way the development sector likes it.

Financialisation of the social housing sector

For a while in the 1990s and 2000s, after council housebuilding was halted by the government, faith was placed by politicians in not-for-profit housing associations providing affordable housing as an alternative. Housing associations were initially supported by generous government grants and were keen to build social and affordable housing at scale. However, this did not last. Government grants to housing associations declined, and in 2015, the Coalition government stopped all direct funding for housing associations. Housing associations become increasingly market oriented, building housing for sale and branching out into commercial development to cross-subsidise the provision of affordable units. They were no longer an agent of social policy. Their story, as we explore later in Chapter 9, is an example of how the social housing sector was sucked into the private developers' world, sadly compromising its original aims and values.

The same dynamic has affected local authorities. As government grants for social and affordable housing have been slashed, local authorities have been encouraged to go into partnership with developers and private landowners. This leads to the ultimate absurdity of public authorities actively pursuing higher values from market-led development in order to find crumbs for social housing development. As the provision of new affordable housing has become dependent on the market, local authorities have entered into risky and one-sided public–private partnerships, often with disastrous social consequences, as when social housing has been demolished and local people rehoused many miles away (Minton, 2017: 53).

The result of this dynamic is that housing has become a tradable asset. This process is known as 'financialisation', whereby housing becomes a financial investment, a means of accumulating personal and corporate wealth. As a consequence, social and affordable housing is measured by its financial value in the marketplace, alongside other housing 'products' such as shared ownership, student housing or Build to Rent. A home has become an asset to be traded or valued as a financial asset for the next generation.

Who benefits?

However, who are the vested interests that benefit most from financialisation and use their influence to make sure that a fairer supply and lower price of housing is blocked? Who benefits from a weakened and demoralised local authority planning system? Who benefits from keeping community-led housing ideas niche and marginalised? Who benefits from stopping more council housing being built? Who are the winners and losers?

Homeowners certainly benefit from rising prices. They have seen the value of houses rise year on year and they are rightly frightened of a fall in prices that might affect their financial security. It was reported in 2018 that the over-65s gained £5.5 billion in property wealth in just one year (*Landlord Today*, 2018). Yet, homeowners do not want their children to be priced out of the housing market, nor do they think that it is desirable to live in a society where there is no accommodation for homeless families, or where there is a demoralised planning system that cannot protect environments and amenities in their own neighbourhoods. Is it not possible to have housing security for themselves and *also at the same time* housing for those in need? Why is it one and not the other?

Homeowners have hopes and fears, but they are not the main blockers to change in the way in which housing development takes place in the UK. The obvious blockers are major landowners, property companies and the property professions who stand to gain from shortages and ever-higher prices. More significantly perhaps, they include a web of banking, finance and investors that is deeply embedded in the fortunes of the land and property market. As we shall see later, the government itself is also a beneficiary with its own vested interest in maintaining the status quo.

How does the finance–housebuilding complex ensure that in spite of well-publicised need, scandalous abuse by landlords and rocketing profits for property and finance company chief executive officers (CEOs) very little is done to build social housing, or bring down house and land prices to make them more affordable? Why is the need for social housing, affordable rents and tenants' rights – even after the catastrophic Grenfell fire of 2017 – not really taken seriously by the government?

The property lobby

A principal reason for the permanency of the housing crisis is the power of the property lobby. The property industry employs a formidable array of consultancy, marketing, academic, legal and property professionals who support commercial and residential development. Landowners and developers pour substantial sums into lobby organisations and political donations. The property lobby has ready access to ministers, using the media to go on the attack against critics, and raising alarm about any real or imagined threat to their power. As we shall see, government has in many ways become part of the property lobby.

The social housing lobby is no match for this access. Although Shelter, Crisis, Generation Rent and the Joseph Rowntree Trust, for example, have thousands of supporters, lobby ministers, produce copious studies of housing need and urge interventions by the government, they get nowhere compared with the commercial property lobby. The property and finance sectors have a level of direct access to the top level of government and the Treasury that far exceeds the social housing lobby. They can be sure that when they talk to ministers, the government will act to protect their market power, whether by deregulation, subsidies or favourable taxation.

This access can be seen in the funding and organisation of the main political parties. Many of their donations and sponsorships come from the finance and property sectors. It is said that half of all donations to the Conservative Party come from the City (Jones, 2014: 268). From a practical housing policy point of view, both the Conservatives and Labour are reliant upon the major housebuilders, landlords and financiers for advice, as well as for delivering government housing targets. Keeping the property lobby onside and in the government tent is a key objective.

Yet, in the business world, many companies are not happy with this state of affairs. In a CBI (Confederation of British Industry) survey of businesses in London in 2018, 66 per cent said that housing costs had a negative effect on the recruitment of entry-level staff and 44 per cent of companies paid premium wages or retention payments to attract staff (Pidd, 2018). But when it comes to a policy choice, the government invariably sides with the property sector not key workers.

A property-dependent economy

If anything, the housing crisis is more complicated and deeper rooted than just the activities of the property sector and their financial backers, or their links to political parties – and the fact that they turn a blind eye to the implications for business. The bigger problem is that property and land in the UK are far more than matters of housing or the state of the environment. The financial value of the finance/property sector literally underpins the whole economy (Ryan-Collins et al, 2017: 160). The implications are sobering. It means that the network of power and influence of the land and property sector affects the whole spectrum of political, cultural and economic issues in the UK (Edwards, 2015: 8). Therefore, housing is not just housing, but also about the sacred British issues of social class, land, wealth and status.

Message of the book

The message of this book is that the housing shortage cannot be tackled without fully understanding, and tackling at source, the pivotal role of finance and the housing development sector and their political networks, which include economic and housing policymakers in the government. Although this power behind housing is known about in general terms, it is so extensive, complex and intimidating that little is done about it. Unless this power is revealed and addressed directly, the housing crisis in the UK will go on indefinitely at huge public expense (in Housing Benefit and in subsidies to housebuilders, landowners and house buyers). Planners and social housing providers at the sharp end of housing need and delivery will have no chance to deliver for their communities unless these structural factors are addressed.

2

The housing shortage

The fallacy of the numbers game

Successive governments and the housebuilding lobby have constructed the housing crisis quite deliberately as a crisis of numbers – and even more narrowly as a lack of housing for sale or housing for first-time buyers. Yes, there is a shortage of new homes, and many first-time buyers are shut out from homeownership; however, the real problem is not the numbers, but the affordability, type, design, quality and location of new and existing homes.

From 2016 onwards, governments have had a target of building at least 300,000 new homes per year in England alone, almost doubling average annual delivery. They believe that if developers are able to build a lot more housing, prices will stabilise, more people will be able to get on the housing ladder and the worst of the housing crisis would effectively be over. However, progress on reaching this target is painfully slow. In 2019, a report by the House of Commons Public Accounts Committee (2019) said that the government was 'way off track' in achieving this target. However, the target itself is disingenuous. If new housing is not affordable, or is not in the right location for those who need it, or is of poor quality, or is unsuitable for the elderly, people with disabilities, young people, the homeless, or those with health problems, then government targets will not help.

The numbers game does not measure how far an increase in the number of new homes meets demand for new housing. Much new supply provided by developers makes no contribution whatsoever to meeting the housing needs of homebuyers or those in housing need. New building, up to 40 per cent in London in the recent boom, was of houses or flats at prices well out of reach of ordinary people. In an article entitled 'Luxury towers wreck cities' Jenkins (2018) cited a report on London housing by Savills, the surveying firm, which found that while 58 per cent of demand was for houses priced at below £450 per square foot, only 20–25 per cent of new homes built in London were at this price. In Zones 1–4 (in central and inner London), no new housing was at this price.

Berkeley Homes, one of the top ten UK builders, built 3,536 homes in 2017. From a government numbers point of view, the company made a decent contribution to meeting the housing shortage. A closer look shows that the average price (note average price) of these homes was £715,000. Berkeley described its homes 'as popular with overseas investors'. Berkeley made £15.1 million profit in 2017 and a total of £2.9 billion profit over the last seven years. The number of homes that Berkeley builds each year contributes nicely to the profits of its shareholders but it does not alleviate the housing crisis.

The decline in affordable housing

Most critically, the numbers game obscures the issue of affordability. In the housing market overall, including both newbuild and existing housing, the affordability of housing has fallen dramatically over the last 15 years. The ratio of house prices to average incomes is an average 8:1, while in major cities, it is 15:1; in parts of the country, it is over 40:1. Symbolically, the highest house price ratio was recorded in the Royal Borough of Kensington and Chelsea, the site of the Grenfell fire tragedy of 2017. Most ordinary folk cannot afford a mortgage or a deposit in these circumstances. Therefore, affordability is far more important than numbers – numbers matter but only if they are connected to genuine affordability.

The Buy to Let boom made things a lot worse. In 1998, 28,700 Buy to Let mortgages were granted; in 2010, this rose to a staggering 1,290,000 (Isaac and O'Leary, 2011: 80). According to a report by Onward, a think tank led by Conservative MP Neil O'Brien, 'Buy to Let landlords have stopped 2.2 million families becoming homeowners' (by taking homes out of the for-sale market and putting them into the rental market). This report is interesting in that it not only puts a number on the impact of the Buy to Let boom, but also indicates fears within the Conservative Party about the potential repercussions of so many people now forced into the private rental market. It notes that renters in marginal seats were paying 10 per cent of their incomes on rent in 1960–80 but 30 per cent from 2000 to 2017 (Kentish, 2018).

Private rents are going off the scale. Rental demand is going up 13 per cent per annum, and supply is falling as some small landlords are pulling out of the market. On average, private rents rose £2,000 per annum between 2010 and 2018, and 1.5 per cent per annum from 2015 while wages stagnated (Da Silva, 2019). Shelter says that in some London boroughs, while rents have jumped 42 per cent since 2011, wages have risen just 2 per cent in the same period. Yet, there is fierce resistance from landlords and the government to rent controls or long-term secure tenancies, arguing that the market will dry up if these measures are introduced. The response of investors is not to tackle the need for cheaper homes, but to take advantage of deregulated tenancies and rents by pouring money into Build to Rent projects at rents that are often way beyond normal levels of affordability. In 2018, CBRE (Coldwell Banker Richard Ellis) research claimed that £31 billion of investment was targeting Build to Rent (Lane, 2019). There are only around 140,000 Build to Rent homes completed or under construction in the UK but the number is expected to rise by 15,000 per annum (CIH, 2018: 15).

Clearly, the lack of affordability and availability of market homes for homeowners and private renters must be addressed by radical action, but this must not obscure the sharp end of the housing crisis, as it has done often in the past. The sharp end, where there is most widespread suffering, is what is happening to the rented social and affordable housing sector. No responsible housing policy can turn its face away from this however many market homes or Build to Rents are built.

The social and affordable housing sector faces a pincer movement of sky-high rents, the loss of social units through Right to Buy, caps on Housing Benefit and a collapse in newbuild social rented housing. This squeeze began to surface in the 1990s but has now accelerated and intensified so that new or existing social rented housing (and specialised housing of all kinds) is becoming like gold dust as the need for it has risen exponentially. Right to Buy has been a disaster for social housing provision and there is no end in sight. The number of council houses stood at 6.5 million in 1980 when Right to Buy began. By 2018, there were just 2 million council homes. Between 2012 and 2018, 12,000 homes per year were sold under Right to Buy and replacement homes were just 1,200 per annum, despite government promises that there would be one-to-one replacement. To rub it in, over 40 per cent of council homes sold were sold to Buy to Let landlords (Collinson, 2017: i). A survey of Right to Buy in London found that 466 companies or individuals own five or more former council-owned properties (Copley, 2019).

The number of new social rented homes from all sources that have been built year on year is pitifully low. For the last few years, it has been around 6,000 per annum; only 5,800 new social rented homes were built in 2017. To put this in context, the Milton Keynes Development Corporation was building 2,000 social rented units *a year* throughout the late 1970s and early 1980s. Crisis, the housing charity, estimates that 90,000 new social rented homes *per year for*

15 years are needed to meet anywhere near the level of demand. This suggests upping the amount of social housing by 12 times over existing levels *every year for 15 years* (Crisis, 2018). In a separate study, Shelter goes further, estimating a need for 3.1 million social homes over 20 years for England alone. It will cost £10 billion a year but will save £60 billion over 30 years in Housing Benefit from reduced rent levels (Shelter, 2018).

Yet, instead of tackling the acute shortage of social rented homes, the government funds private landlords via the Housing Benefit system to provide housing for those who cannot afford to buy, to the tune of over £22 billion a year (Johnson, 2019). How many social homes could that sum build? Such is the resistance of the government to investing in a large-scale council house-building programme, or putting substantial funding into social homes provided by charitable bodies, that they would rather support poor-quality and expensive private rented housing than provide decent secure affordable housing. This harsh politics is not sound public economics.

The 'affordability' label is now meaningless

Part of the deep frustration with how housing is tackled by the government is that the very word 'affordable' in housing-speak has become 'Orwellian'. It is presented as something reasonable and sensible when included in government guidance or from the mouths of housing ministers seeking to alleviate people's fears. A closer examination shows that the government definition of 'affordable rent', at 80 per cent of local market rent, is not affordable to most people in housing need across large swathes of the country, particularly in London, the South East and big cities. For example, the government announced in a fanfare in 2018 that 41,530 affordable homes were built in England in 2016–17, but below the headline, the detail showed that only 5,380 (or 13 per cent) were for social rent, 24,350 were for 'affordable rent' and 11,810 were for 'intermediate rent'.

There are some signs that the message about the meaningless of 'affordability' is getting through. In 2017, the government talked openly of a 'broken housing market'. The prime minister made bold announcements regarding tackling social renting and 'eliminate rough sleeping with in a decade'. *The Times* newspaper headline on 31 January 2018 was 'Greedy house developers face losing right to build' (Sylvester, 2018). In the autumn of 2018, before the Conservative Party annual conference and in the midst of the Brexit crisis, the government made a flurry of new announcements about housing, but a closer look again reveals no change in policy. The first lot of announcements were of the usual kind, for example, more subsidy programmes for housebuilders to help them out with infrastructure costs and reduce their risks, including a £2 billion kick-start fund for small sites and £1.3 billion for land assembly. Typically, no conditions were attached to this fund in order to ensure social housing, good planning or the relaxation of the Right to Buy.

The same mixed messaging applies to Treasury announcements that the borrowing cap on local authorities will be lifted, potentially allowing them to borrow in order to build affordable housing for the first time in many years. The lifting of the cap has been demanded by local authorities and community housing groups for many years, with the government turning a deaf ear even as the housing crisis deepened. Then, in 2018, the Chancellor of the Exchequer announced that the cap would be lifted. This could have been a significant moment depending on the detailed conditions attached, for example, which authorities could qualify, how much could be borrowed and whether the Right to Buy would apply. Predictably, the conditions were restrictive and did not include removing the Right to Buy for new homes. It became clear that the effect of lifting the cap was overblown. Original estimates were that lifting the cap could enable 10,000–15,000 extra affordable homes a year to be built in England, but the Office for Budget Responsibility estimated that the figure was more likely to be only 4,000 a year over the next five years and a net increase of only 9,000 over five years (Barratt, 2018a). Given that Crisis says that we need 90,000 extra social units per year, removing the cap clearly does not go anywhere near far enough.

Despite the previous eight years of governments stigmatising migrants and social housing tenants, in 2018, the prime minister unexpectedly criticised those who demonised social housing tenants and announced a new funding package. This could be seen as a cynical move at the height of the Brexit crisis and a response to the government's public relations (PR) disaster over the causes and consequences of the Grenfell fire. Nevertheless, the funding announcement was greeted warmly by the housing association sector, though, strangely, no one asked what the strings attached were, for example, would Right to Buy be lifted? Would secure tenancies be allowed? Was the funding for 'starter homes' or for social housing? It looked very much like useful political spin at a critical time. If not, was the offer another hidden subsidy for the housebuilders, enabling them to sell unsold units en bloc to housing associations as they knew that housing associations now had a sudden cash injection to buy unsold units?

One of the pervasive myths trotted out by ministers, developers and some academics is that building more houses will bring down house prices. Alarm over spiralling house prices in the 2000s boom, and again in the 2012–18 boom, led to claims by both academics and volume builders that building a lot more housing, for example, by letting development take place on green belt land or reducing planning regulations, would eventually bring down prices to more 'sustainable levels'.

In 2004, the New Labour government commissioned economist Kate Barker (2004) to examine the contention that building a lot more homes would bring down prices. She concluded that if you built an additional 250,000 new homes per annum, it would bring down prices by just 1 per cent. Given that newbuild housing accounts for only a small fraction of housing on the market (6 per cent) and second-hand homes set the general level of prices nationally, this is not surprising. Yet, in spite of this evidence, the government and the property lobby have continued to trot out the argument that increasing supply would bring down or stabilise prices and increase affordability. The self-interest of the landowners and builders is clear: the property lobby needs the concept of shortage to persuade the government and local authorities to make more land available through the planning system. This process is examined more closely in Chapter 3.

Perhaps, just perhaps, even if there is no change in policy on affordable housing, there is a change of tone in some quarters over the blame game and some acknowledgement in the government that it is not the planners in local government who are responsible for the small numbers of new homes built. In 2017, the government set up an investigation led by Sir Oliver Letwin MP into why housebuilders build out their developments so slowly, even where they own the land and have plentiful planning consents. After years of hotly denying that they would ever do such a thing as 'drip-feed' housing onto the market, the housebuilders were being asked to account for their role in the broken housing market.

Whether these government announcements and investigations will effect real change in how the shortage is defined, or in building housing for those in need – and whether it means the property lobby is diminished as a result – we return to in more detail later. At this point, it is worth saying that government housing announcements since 2017 suggest that housing is now finally on the political agenda and even Conservative governments are looking slightly more critically at how the housing supply market works. However, is there progress where it matters — in an honest understanding of what has caused the crisis and in action to deal with it?

Taking the long view

Questions about affordability, the volume housebuilders' intentions and government policy appear immediately pressing, but in order to understand them more fully, it is useful to take the long view of the housing crisis and housing shortage. How have we come to this point and what would it take to turn it around?

Housing shortages are not new. They have changed their character and political visibility many times, from the need for post-war rebuilding, to the demand for homes to buy, to the refurbishment of council homes and to the shortage of social rented housing. However, one trend is unmistakable over the last 40 years. The state, mainly the government and local authorities, has a less direct role in building and managing housing, while the private sector has a much larger role in building, in setting rents and in housing management. This has happened because the government has switched its funding and support for new building and public housing renewal from the public sector to the private housebuilders. In the meantime, the public and not-for-profit housing sectors have been left with the responsibility, but not the funding, to provide housing for those on very low incomes, and specialised housing for the elderly, the homeless and those with health needs.

In the post-war period, the concept of shortages was stark: there was an urgent need for reconstruction and the demolition of slum housing. The government had to act and did. The new towns and overspill town programmes of the post-war period were government interventions in housing provision on a massive scale. Under the New Towns Act 1946, 29 new towns were designated, housing 1.4 million by 1970. Alongside this, over 500,000 people were accommodated in designated overspill towns around the big cities (Hall, 1973: 333). More new towns and expansion towns followed in the 1960s and 1970s, including the largest and most successful, Milton Keynes, which was designated in 1967.

In terms of new housebuilding, the now well-known chart in Figure 1 of new housebuilding by councils, the private market and housing associations from 1946 to 2019 shows the rise of council housebuilding until the late 1970s and its sharp fall afterwards. There was an increase of housing association building from the 1990s. It is noteworthy that the level of contribution of newbuild homes from private housebuilders, approximately 150,000 per annum from the mid-1960s to the present, has changed very little over the last 40 years, and has not compensated for the fall in council supply. This flatlining persisted even after volume housebuilders were heavily subsidised by successive governments, more land was granted planning permission for housing and mortgage rates for homebuyers were held at historically low levels. The reasons for this contradiction – more government support for volume housebuilding but no more housing built – lies at the heart of this book, and is examined later in Chapter 3.

Thus, in the recent history of housing in the UK, there have been two critical turning points. The first was 1946, which began large-scale central and local government intervention in council housebuilding in the post-war period. The second was 1980, when the government abandoned the post-war public housing strategy and fully embraced private sector building. Post-1980, the state transferred more and more of its housing budget to the private sector and to Housing Benefit. This is the period when the Right to Buy for council homes came in, homeownership was promoted as the gold standard for social mobility, the new towns programme was halted and private housebuilders were offered generous subsidies. The year 1980 was also the beginning of a concerted attack by central government on the powers and funding of local authorities. Given that local authorities were the main developers and managers of housing in the post-war period, this policy change was a major blow to national housing provision. It also switched the characterisation of the national housing crisis epitomised in the 'Cathy Come Home' Shelter campaign of the 1960s (and the film of the same name by Ken Loach) from a concern for homelessness to a concern

Figure 1: Housebuilding by tenure, England, 1946–2017

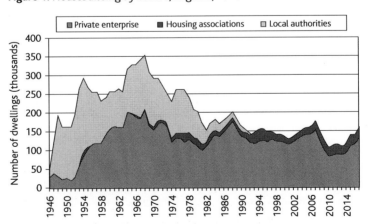

Source: MHCLG, 2019b

for homeownership. Thus, post-1980, successive governments have seen homeowners as their main political constituency, not those in housing need at the bottom of the pile.

The year 1980 was also the moment when the housebuilding sector, on the back of the switch in government housing priorities, evolved from small builders to corporate giants. Some may recall that Margaret Thatcher was a big fan of Lawrie Barratt, founder of Barratt Developments, and his helicopter. Barratt Developments is now the UK's largest housebuilder. The growth of the volume builders will be examined in Chapter 3.

The rise of the volume housebuilders came about because homeowners and potential homebuyers have been the priority group for successive governments, who have pressed local authorities to allocate more land for housing for sale, and have driven this forward by imposing national and local housing targets (King, 2006). For developers and landowners, the political drive to homeownership is a gift that keeps on giving simply because as the principal owners of housing development land, they are able to capture most of the benefits of massive increases in land value as their sites are zoned for housing.

The trend of reduced direct state provision and reliance on the land and property market to deliver new homes has now persisted for nearly 40 years. It has taken place in spite of a surge in demand for affordable housing from households of all sizes, and the evident need for housing for the elderly, disabled, single people and those with special needs. This growing diversity of demand is nowhere near matched by a diversity of supply. Huge areas of demand are largely unmet by the state or not-for-profit sectors because they do not have the funding or capacity, meaning that those who are poor or on low incomes, including those who are disabled or mentally ill, are thrown into the overpriced private rented sector, or into risky mortgage arrangements – or onto the streets.

Estate regeneration

Another factor reducing the stock of social housing is 'estate regeneration'. Estate regeneration is the physical remodelling of council estates and the introduction of a new 'tenure mix' in the new development. Local authorities enter into development partnerships with property companies, trading in their land and buildings in return for public and private finance for regeneration. The partnership deals are based on a profit-making strategy, where social rented homes are replaced by market housing, 'shared ownership' or 'intermediate rents', with only a paltry number of social homes in the shiny new developments. The examples of the Aylesbury Estate regeneration in Southwark[1] and Woodberry Down in Hackney are typical, and have been investigated in detail by community groups and campaigning journalists like Chakrabortty (2014) who has written about the disastrous partnership between Hackney Council and Berkeley Homes at Woodberry Down.

Two reasons are usually given to justify such transformations of council estates: first, private partnerships reduce the public sector costs of refurbishment; and, second, there are social benefits from a mix of tenures on large estates. However, the partnerships, as Chakrabortty has shown, have come at the price of selling off public assets, forcing out existing tenants, creating value that is taken out of the community by developers and losing large numbers of social rented homes that have to be provided elsewhere (or not at all). As for the social benefits of a mix of tenures, this might be a more believable argument if the balance of market versus social homes in regenerated estates was determined by detailed social planning rather than development accountants.

Many tenants point out that if a community- or local authority-led ownership model of regeneration was used instead, council estates could be renewed without reducing the stock of affordable housing or by forcing out existing tenants. In Newham, East London, the People's Empowerment Alliance for Custom House (PEACH) has developed just such a community-led model for the regeneration of their estate near the Royal Docks. This model showed that if the local authority did not sell the land to a developer, but regenerated the estate *with* the community in a public–civic partnership that retained land value in the community, there would be a much higher level of social housing and a more balanced tenure mix. Moreover, regeneration would be more locally accountable and the existing community could stay together (PEACH, 2018). For the future of Custom House, much depends on how the local authority, Newham Council, responds to this eminently feasible proposal.

What about quality?

It is not just the quantity of new housing that is in short supply, but also the quality. Despite rising demands for greater energy efficiency and more space, quite apart from the NPPF principle of sustainable development, new homes built by the volume housebuilders are notoriously cramped and poorly built compared with our major European neighbours. The volume housebuilders are always keen to publicise their consumer surveys, which usually show a high proportion of satisfied customers on their new estates. Yet, research has shown that the private house building industry is producer rather than consumer-led. One study concluded that 'what is clear from study results is the fact that the housebuilder industry has only limited ability to respond to the evident diversity in housebuyers tastes and preferences' (Leishman and Warren, 2005: 184). Over the longer term, UK volume-built homes have shrunk in size by 20 per cent since the 1970s, with smaller living rooms and bedrooms, smaller windows, less storage and smaller gardens compared with almost every other European country; yet, they have gone up much higher in price than their continental counterparts (Garber, 2018).

Newbuild customers are pleased to get a home under the circumstances of acute shortages in the UK, but the quality could and should be a lot better. The reason that it is not, is that land is absurdly expensive. UK housebuilders focus on packing homes on sites, and maximising unit profit rather than maximising the quality of provision. Local authorities and regulators have allowed the builders to do this, with minimal protest from the town planning or building control professions. The government has belatedly suggested that there will be a 'new homes ombudsman' but it is no surprise to discover that it is formulating this proposal with the Home Builders Federation (HBF). Whatever watered-down proposals come out will no doubt be welcome for processing consumer complaints but will be no use at all for dealing with the shrinking size of new homes.

Geography of shortages

The geography of shortages in England is striking and enduring. The greatest shortages of all types of housing are in high-value areas of London and across the South East, but there are also shortages of social/affordable and specialised housing right across the country, with acute shortages of good-quality social housing in all the larger cities. Rural areas, villages and small towns also have their own housing crises, as evidenced by the plethora of neighbourhood plans in villages and rural parishes in England that want more social and affordable housing in order to keep young people and key workers, and to provide for the elderly in village communities. No area, however apparently wealthy, is exempt from a housing crisis of some kind.

Governments and academic commentators have claimed that one of the main reasons for the intricate geography of housing shortages is Nimbyism on the part of local authorities and local communities. Yet, environmental groups such as the Campaign to Protect Rural

England (CPRE) argue that much of this Nimbyism is justified if it means protecting the green belt and other special sites. They say that there is more than enough brownfield land available for development if only the housebuilders would choose to build on it (CPRE, 2018).

At a local level, many community groups argue that much new housing is in the wrong location, is badly designed or planned, or has no amenities. Often, it is too expensive to meet local needs. These are perfectly valid and rational objections. To dismiss them all as Nimbyism is to let the housebuilders, the landowners and the planners off the hook. The developers, working with the planners, should be providing better-quality homes and a more carefully planned distribution of housing. Neighbourhood plans are showing that fine-grained local knowledge is a much better guide to how and what housing development should take place in local communities than following the standard housebuilders' model (Brownill and Bradley, 2017).

Conclusion

The persistent shortages of housing and escalating lack of affordability over the last 20 years appear to be hard-wired into UK housing policy, in particular, into housing policy in England. There are multiple changes of housing ministers and frequent policy initiatives but nothing seems to change for the better. There are three unmistakable long-term trends: first, the government depends on the private sector to deliver new housing, with affordable housing depending on spin-offs from private development; second, volume housebuilders depend on the government to support them; and, third, local authorities have now been drawn into cross-subsidy through participation in public–private partnerships for major developments on their own land, including estate regeneration, leading to the loss of thousands of social and affordable units and the break-up of communities.

The argument about why there are housing shortages comes back to two conspiracy theories: the first, from the social housing sector, is that landowners, developers and the government are deliberately not building enough new housing to keep up prices; the second, from the finance–housebuilding complex, is that local authority planners and Nimbys are imposing unreasonable restrictions on developers. One thing is certain: the government has tried to collapse all housing needs – housing for sale, affordable housing and social housing – into one box which says that the private sector will sort this out. Anyone who criticises this approach is somehow 'not living in the real world'.

Of course, this is not true and makes no economic, environmental or social sense.

If we look only at housing for sale, as Figure 1 shows, even when everything has been in their favour – government financial and political support, the ownership of vast acreages of development land, low interest rates for long periods and plentiful planning consents – the volume housebuilders have failed to build enough housing decade after decade. Moreover, much of what is built is of poor quality in terms of specifications, space standards and neighbourhood amenities. It is not difficult to understand why developers and landowners do not want to build social and affordable housing: it reduces land costs and developer profits. But why do they not bring their land banks forward if it means that they can sell more market housing? This critical question, which goes to heart of their business model (and to the related business models of financiers, investors and landowners), is the subject of Chapter 3.

3

The housebuilding business

When Peter Ambrose and I wrote a book called *The property machine* back in 1975 looking at developers in the UK and their impact on local communities, national housebuilding companies were a little-known part of the property industry, and even less of the investment market (Ambrose and Colenutt, 1975). In those days, the big developers, backed with institutional finance (pension funds and insurance companies), were office developers such as Land Securities, Hammerson and British Land. The commercial property market (or commercial real estate as it is now called) has since then hugely expanded and diversified into retail, leisure and, more recently, residential development.

As private housebuilding for sale has become increasingly important to the government and consumers, the major housebuilding developers have become more corporate and closely integrated with the finance sector. They are now 'volume builders' who have absorbed dozens of smaller builders and their land banks. They are listed on the stock exchange and play an important part in the fortunes of the investment market.

Fred Wellings, the pre-eminent chronicler of the housebuilders, describes an industry of individual builder entrepreneurs until the 1970s. It evolved through a process of consolidation and takeover, 'driven by financial opportunism, the influence of the Stock Exchange and personal motivation' (Wellings, 2006: 3). Over a fairly short period of time, the major housebuilders were able to capture a large part of the market. In 2018, the top ten builders built 30 per cent of all new homes in the UK, and these companies are getting bigger and bigger and more powerful in the market. Those building over 2,000 homes per year built 63 per cent of new homes in 2017 (Savills, 2018). The top ten UK housebuilders are: Barratt, Taylor Wimpey, Bellway, Persimmon, Berkeley, Galliford Try, Redrow, Crest Nicholson, Bovis and Countryside (*Housebuilder*, 2018).

Table 1, comparing the top ten housebuilders in 2000 with the top ten housebuilders in 2016, tells a story of major names being absorbed into other companies. Several major household names such as McAlpine and David Wilson have disappeared, being taken over or merged with others, notably, Barratt, Persimmon and Taylor Wimpey. Meanwhile, the number of units built by the largest companies has risen significantly over the 15-year period.

Table 1: Top ten housebuilders, 2000 and 2016

2000: top ten companies	2000: units built	2016: top ten companies	2016: units built	2016: operating profit (£ million)
Barratt	10,636	Barratt	17,319	668
Beazer	8,223	Taylor Wimpey	13,881	744
Persimmon	7,035	Persimmon	15,171	720
Bellway	5,714	Bellway	8,721	492
Westbury	4,435	Berkeley	3,776	451
Wilcon	4,215	Redrow	4,716	261
McAlpine	4,007	Galliford Try	3,604	159
Brant	3,461	Bovis	3,997	160
David Wilson	2,604	Crest Nicholson	2,870	204
Bloor Homes	2,000	L&Q	2,552	115
Total	**50,330**		**73,737**	

Source: Wellings, 2006: 104, 180, Table 6.1, Table 7.1 and Concentration Table 10.2; and *Housebuilder*, 2017.

The mid–2000s boom was the takeover era: Persimmon bought Westbury for £643 million; Galliford Try bought Linden Homes for £243 million; and Barratt bought Wilson Homes for a staggering £2.3 billion. The biggest merger of all was between Taylor Woodrow and Wimpey in 2007, which was worth £5 billion. Government ministers became alarmed at the scale of consolidation, but merger activity started again after the 2008 financial crash. In the 2012–18 boom, both Galliford Try and Redrow attempted to take over Bovis Homes. Then in 2019 Bovis bought Galliford Try and Linden Homes for £1.1 billion.

With their domination of the market, the operating margins of the six largest housebuilding firms rose sharply because they were in a position to take advantage of the property boom post-2012. For the top six, margins were on average 3 per cent in 2009, but by 2016, they were over 20 per cent (*Housebuilder*, 2017). In their annual report for 2017, Persimmon announced that their operating margin was up to 28 per cent and profits were up 25 per cent from 2013. In 2017, Bellway announced margins of 22 per cent and profits up 16 per cent on the previous year. The country's largest housebuilder, Barratt, completed 17,579 homes in the year to June 2018, with pre-tax profit jumping 9 per cent to a record £835 million and with operating margins at 17.7 per cent. Operating profits for the housebuilding sector as whole rose by 21 per cent in 2017/18. In 2017, the top ten housebuilders produced 27,000 more homes than five years earlier (*Housebuilder*, 2018). Barratt has said that it aims to grow volumes by 3–5 per cent in the medium term and added that it has the capacity to build 20,000 homes a year.

This growth has created personal fortunes for the CEOs of the big housebuilders. A dramatic example was the extraordinary £85 million bonus payout to Jeff Fairburn, former CEO of Persimmon, on the back of a 20 per cent rise in company profits in 2017. The group managing director who took over from Fairburn in 2018 got a bonus of £45 million. The chairman of Berkeley Homes, Tony Pidgley, received a personal payout of £48 million in 2018 following a previous payout of £23 million in 2015 when company profits rose 42 per cent. At the same time, Berkeley has consistently reduced its affordable housing obligations on homes built in London claiming that affordable housing targets are 'unviable' (Neale et al, 2018).

However, it is not just the distribution of profits to a tiny number of executives that is so shocking; it is the political influence that goes with it. There is little doubt that personal financial success gives greater leverage for the big housebuilders in Whitehall. As an example, Tony Pidgley of Berkeley Homes was a member of Heseltine's Estate Regeneration Advisory Panel and advised the government on the disposal of public sector land. He received a CBE from Prime Minister David Cameron in 2012 and a series of gifts from Boris Johnson, the Mayor of London at that time. In a moment of extreme irony, the Berkeley Group received the Queen's Award for Sustainable Development in 2014. An article in *Property Wire* reported that in return Pidgley gave a donation to the Conservative Party and wrote to the *Daily Telegraph* before the 2015 general election expressing his support for the Conservatives, citing their housing and development policies (Rowntree, 2016).

The rise in profits and personal fortunes was not caused by company expertise; rather, it was fuelled by government subsidy through Help to Buy, by loans and grants from the Homes and Communities Agency (now Homes England), and by planning deregulation that enabled housebuilders to avoid building affordable housing. It was widely reported that Help to Buy had directly inflated the salaries and bonuses of housing executives such as those at Persimmon where nearly half of their house sales in 2018 were funded in part by Help to Buy (Neale, 2019; Baynes, 2019).

Indeed, as a result of this financial success, the housebuilding sector has become increasingly attractive to major investment funds.[1] In the 2012–18 housing boom, investor magazines were strongly recommending investment in large housebuilders, citing high-performing shares and government commitment to housebuilding. One example of overseas investment in the UK housebuilding sector was the announcement in 2018 that a Malaysian company, EcoWorld, had bought a 70 per cent stake in Willmott Dixon, one of the largest construction and development companies in the UK, in a deal worth £2.5 billion (Crane, 2017).

This property-driven investment boom is high risk. As I write, in the feverish climate of Brexit negotiations, there are multiple warnings that the market in London has peaked, with prices of more expensive properties generally falling sharply. Nevertheless, these same investors are expecting that if Brexit is resolved luxury housing in London will take off again because of the amount of pent-up demand for this type of property (Gerrity, 2019).

The business model

Although there are as many business strategies as there are types of housebuilders, all housebuilders employ the same basic business model (Payne, 2015). The success of this model has driven the growth and consolidation in the sector, as well as the continued rise in profits in the recent boom period. Protecting and enhancing this model is the central concern of the property industry in its relationship with the government.

The principal objective of a housebuilding company is to make a profit for its shareholders. To do this, the value of each individual development, or a portfolio of developments, must be more than the costs of developing and building the project. The same objective applies to the company as a whole: the value created and realised in the market must be more than overall costs. Value creation and value capture from this process are the central aims of the housebuilding company and its financial backers. In practice, the business relies on a pipeline of land, part of which is sold or traded, and part of which is developed in a way that 'creates value' from the land and the completed development. The bread and butter of the land-trading side of the business is to buy land cheap and sell on at the right time.

The development side of this business model is the cost and profit equation for each potential development site. The key variables in this equation are:

- the profit margin;
- the land costs;

- the costs of finance;
- the costs of construction;
- the costs of fees to architects, surveyors and lawyers, and for marketing;
- the level of subsidies that can be obtained from central or local government (for example, for mortgage holders, infrastructure or affordable housing);
- the value of the completed development (rents, house sales and sales of land parcels);
- payments to the local authority for community facilities or physical infrastructure such as roads, often known as Section 106 or Community Infrastructure Levy (CIL) payments.

We need to look at the politically sensitive parts of this equation to understand on which issues lobbying and policy blockages are most significant.

Profit margin

The profit margin is a key number in the business model because it is the target scheme profit for the developer. The development sector usually applies a minimum 20 per cent profit (or mark-up) on value as an 'industry standard' level of profit. This target level of profit is much higher than most economic sectors. The reason given for this by the industry and the banks is that property development is 'high risk' compared with other sectors. The risks cited are: the large upfront costs in land acquisition and construction; long lead times before a development is completed; uncertainty over planning decisions; and vulnerability to booms and slumps. However, this risk is often exaggerated. Sir John Callcutt, who was asked by the government to conduct a major review of the housebuilding sector in 2007 (during the 2000s boom), concluded that 'Investors assume high risks whatever the state of the market' (Callcutt, 2007: 22). In other words, they seek a high level of mark-up profit whatever the actual level of risk.

Academic studies of the sector have reached the same conclusion. Andrew Baum (2015: 21), an expert in property investment, suggests that property investors are generally risk-averse and conservative, and that property investment is, in fact, a low- to medium-risk investment. This makes sense given unlimited demand for housing over the medium term, and given that developers build in an insurance of 20 per cent profit when they value their developments. Indeed, the 20 per cent profit guarantee pretty much removes the risk to developers and their financiers – as if by magic. Sometimes, developers even call their share their 'protected profit' – would that communities could claim that their share of affordable housing from major development was also 'protected'. It helps a lot that landowners do not challenge this level of developer profit because landowners themselves are making an even greater windfall profit from the sale of their land to developers.

In fact, there is little published information on individual landowner profits. Housing campaign groups have tried to estimate the overall level of profit that landowners have received from obtaining planning consents for housing. The answer is astonishing. The National Housing Federation estimates that in 2016/17, landowners in England made £13 billion in profit from land sales (up from £9 billion in 2014/15), more than double the total profits of Amazon, McDonald's and Coca-Cola put together (National Housing Federation, 2018).

Landowner profit is not the only reason why housing development risk is grossly exaggerated. Quite apart from benefitting from consistent high levels of demand for housing, the modern housebuilding company is not a fly-by-night operation. Expert reviews of the housebuilding industry, such as by Callcutt, demonstrate that risk management is well established. Developers maintain close links with their financiers and operate careful scheme portfolio management. Most importantly, they maintain large land banks that provide a secure rising-in-value asset base. Clearly, in parts of the country where demand is high, the risks are lower than in low-demand areas – as is proven by the increase in the margins of the big builders and investors who have heavily concentrated their building and land acquisition in London and South East over the past 20 years.

In this context, the application of a standard industry profit for developers across a diverse range of development schemes in different parts of the country with varied levels of risk is impossible to justify. Academic studies have concluded that estimating a required rate of return from a property development requires data that do not exist or assumptions that are difficult to verify (Crosby et al, 2017). This is not just of academic interest. The developer profit target is an estimate of risk and if this risk is overestimated, perhaps deliberately, then less land value is available for affordable housing obligations. Thus, industry assumptions about profits built into their viability models have a direct impact on communities.

Some local authorities and communities have tried to challenge industry standard conventions at planning inquiries into affordable housing, suggesting that, in many cases, a lower profit margin of 12–15 per cent on value does not threaten viability – and would allow more of the value created by a new development to be directed to affordable housing and community facilities.[2] Yet, despite these arguments by objectors, many consultants advising clients have refused to budge from the 20 per cent guideline. But cracks are appearing; recent government guidance on viability assessment for Local Plans says 'plan makers may choose to apply alternative figures where there is evidence to support this' and suggest a range of 15 to 20 per cent (GOV.UK, 2019).

It is worth adding that the actual profits from many residential land developments can be very much higher than 20 per cent, ranging from 20 per cent to 40 per cent. Thus, while developers complain that they will suffer if profits fall below the 20 per cent standard, they are privately expecting much higher out-turn profits than that – and their investors expect this to be so. Typically, when developers pitch to their investors, they say that they can achieve high levels of profit, but when they negotiate with local authorities, they say that the scheme is barely viable and any further planning obligations will kill off the scheme. Therefore, there is no doubt that the argument for a standard profit when negotiating social and affordable housing contributions is part of gaming the system.

Fees

In addition to developers and landowners taking a big share of the value created by new housing development, a large number of professionals, consultants and agencies also expect a share. They include surveyors, architects, lawyers, marketing agencies and land agencies. Their fees are usually based on a percentage of the development value or the development costs, which can range from 3 per cent to 12 per cent depending on the role that they are taking.

Cumulatively, professional fees take a very big chunk of the value created by development, further shrinking the amount that is available for community benefits or affordable housing. For the professionals and agencies, the larger the cost and value of the development, the greater the return to them, giving little reason to support regulation that might make land values or house prices cheaper or more affordable. Hence, their professional bodies and lobby groups, such as the RICS (see later), have every reason to support the status quo and lobby hard to make sure that this is so. It should be noted that the local authority planners and housing officers who deal with planning applications and negotiate with developers and their advisers over affordable housing do not benefit from the increase in values since their salaries are fixed by local government scales while the fees for the professionals working for the developers are not.

Land valuation

Land is the central component in housing development because the land price accounts for so much of the value in housebuilding. Land can comprise 50–70 per cent of the value of a house. While a big slice of development value is taken by the developers, associated contractors and professionals, the largest chunk of the profit from housing development is taken by the previous landowner.

For the developer to obtain his share of the uplift in value, he must acquire land at the right time, in the right place and at the right price. If the developer pays too much for the land, he will not be able to deliver all the elements of the scheme that he has promised. If the developer offers too little, the landowner will not sell. The objective of the developer is to maximise land value uplift from his development, that is, the difference between the purchase price of the land and the value of the land with the new development on it. The landowner is in a different position. The objective of the landowner is to give away in negotiation as little of the uplift in value as he can allow while ensuring that the developer does not walk away. This is why land valuation (and negotiation) is the key professional process in residential land development. Both developer and landowner have a big stake in getting the valuation they want – and this has implications for local communities.

The most commonly used method of land valuation is the residual valuation method. In summary, the residual land value is the difference between the market value of the completed development and the costs including the developer's profit. This is far from a technical or objective assessment. Each component of the valuation (profit margins, fees, finance, prices, government grants and Section 106 or CIL payments to local authorities) varies over time and across locations. Many are contested matters, involving negotiation with landowners, financiers, the government and local authorities. None of the outcomes are fixed or clearly known at the outset. Although chartered surveyors and land economists sometimes like to tell us that land valuation is a formula it is political. There are the obvious political inputs such as town planning rules, government grants and government guidance over viability, and there is also the less visible power that landowners and developers have in the process of negotiation. Political values and social influence as our case studies will show have a major bearing on the numbers that come out of the valuation equation.

The subjectivity of valuation is no longer seriously in question. One of the most heavyweight textbooks on property investment questions the accuracy of property valuations, concluding that 'there is a consensus that individual valuations are prone to a degree of uncertainty' (Baum, 2015: 11). This is putting it mildly. In practice, standard valuation concepts such as market value, existing use value or threshold land value (the price at which a landowner is prepared to sell), which are the foundations of land valuation, are hotly debated and are subject to critical examination at planning inquiries and tribunals. Not surprisingly, academic studies have shown that valuations of the same project vary widely between different valuation professionals (Crosby et al, 2017).

One specialist commentator, Mick Beaman, has some quotes on his website that sum up the inaccuracy of residual valuations and the lack of wisdom of anyone relying on them: 'Once valuers are let loose on residual valuations, however honest the valuers and however reasoned their argument, they can prove almost anything'.[3] He cites the case of Staughton LJ in *Nykredit Mortgage Bank plc v Edward Erdman Group Ltd* [1996] where the court was shown five different residual valuations of the same site (carried out by leading firms): 'By taking the highest and the lowest figure from the five one could arrive at residual site values of either £4,734,422 or £65,666 which, as Euclid would say, is absurd.'[4]

Beaman concludes that 'If a system for land value capture is to work – and I hope it does – it must not be based on the use of residual land valuation models to test viability. As a methodology it is just not good enough and much too easy to manipulate.'[5] Yet, this is the very methodology that is the foundation of the all-important viability assessment determining the amount of affordable housing that developers build under Section 106 obligations. The implications of this are explored in detail in Chapter 6.

The professional body for valuers and chartered surveyors, the RICS, purports to arbitrate between the various stakeholders and set professional standards over property valuation. It publishes its own *Red book* guidelines and rules for land and property valuation (RICS, 2017). Yet, at the same time, the RICS is a policy lobby group for the profession. Most of the time, its members act on the side of the landowner/developer sector rather than local authorities or communities because that is where the majority of their client fees come from. Moreover, the market-led nature of the UK development market means that this is the side that they lean towards in relation to valuation rules and lobbying on policy. Are they biased? Yes, probably – and inevitably. We look at this contention in Chapter 5.

Land banks

Acquiring a bank of land for development or onward sale is the underpinning of the housebuilding industry. Three types of land are held by the large development companies:

- short-term land that has outline planning consent;
- medium-term land that has planning consent pending; and
- strategic land that does not yet have clear planning status.

Strategic land makes up by far the largest percentage of a company's land bank. It is the central speculative process in the housebuilding industry. Strategic land is defined as land owned or controlled by the housebuilder and is normally held under option for development in the future. An option is a contract between a developer and a landowner by which a developer will pay a fee to the landowner to give the developer first option for a specific period of time to bring forward the development of the site. The housebuilder (or land promoter) will seek to get the site classified by the planning authority as potential housing development land and will seek planning consent from the local authority. If they succeed, then the landowner will be bound to sell to the housebuilder or land promoter under the option agreement, who can and often does sell on. The option agreement gives the developer certainty that if they get consent, they can capture most of the increase in land value after having bought from the landowner at the price agreed in the original option contract (Short et al, 1986).

This process has been continuing for many years, such that most potential housing land around major cities and towns in England is held under option to developers or land promoters or traders. In a case study of housebuilding in Berkshire in 1986, the researchers found that almost all potential development sites were secured by the large housebuilders before the formal local plan designation was announced (Short et al, 1986: 54). The large companies and land-trading groups work out the best locations to buy land and purchase development options for short-term development, and to assemble their strategic land portfolios. The search process is thorough and systematic, and relies on very close relationships with the local authority planning system. Similar strategies were employed by housebuilders in studies by Adams (1984) of developers trying to influence the Ashford Local Plan and the Surrey Heath Local Plan.

Since the 1980s, the search process has become much more systematic and employs more surveyors and land agents. Landowners working with housebuilders or land promoters lobby local authorities to get their land allocated for housing and have the inside track on potential land designations by meeting with local authority planning officers or politicians. Whichever way it is done, housing site designations in local plans reflect landowner and developer pressures more than anything else. As Adams (1984: 110) put it after his study of developers and local plan preparation: 'The preparation of statutory local plans presents well informed housebuilders in an area with an opportunity to influence the supply of development land for some years to come.'

Currently, the top six UK housebuilding companies own or control 300,000 short-term plots, equating to five years' supply at current rates of output (*Housebuilder*, 2018: Graph 7). Behind those numbers lie double that amount of plots in strategic land banks, amounting to at least ten years' supply. Each year, more land is acquired. For example, in 2016/17, the top six housebuilders acquired 150,000 plots between them. Over the last ten years, the top ten housebuilders have acquired over 2 million plots of development land, demonstrating the scale of their control over the residential land market in the UK. Furthermore, as company ownership has become more concentrated, with a greater ownership of development land in a few hands, the large volume housebuilders have correspondingly greater influence over local and national politicians, and their civil servants, who make policy on planning and housebuilding.

The pace of corporate land acquisition is alarming and accelerating, particularly within the South East. Grosvenor Estates, for example, once a traditional landed estates business, has branched out into new development projects. It recently announced that it is planning to triple the size of its strategic land business, targeting a pipeline of 30,000 new homes in five years. The sites are all in the South East of England, 'within striking distance of London' (Dransfield, 2018).

The imperative of land acquisition and control has not only driven the volume builders to greater and greater levels of site search and land acquisition. In addition, there is an industry of land promoters looking for sites speculatively or on behalf of client housebuilders, undertaking preliminary planning work enabling them to sell on. According to a study by Lichfield consultants on behalf of the Land Promoters and Developers Federation (LPDF) (for more on the LPDF, see Chapter 5), specialist land promoters undertake 50 per cent of all the work on pre-application sites across the country (Lichfield Consultants, 2018). In other words, land promoters are driving much of the national accumulation of land banks on behalf of major developers and institutions. The local implications of this land grab are evident everywhere. For example, a recent study of development land around Swindon showed that because most land on the outskirts of the town had been acquired by land promoters for residential development, local authorities were 'unable to resist unplanned housing development' and there is little land left over for lower-value industrial development (Holly, 2018).

Furthermore, if they do not succeed in their initial submissions to have their sites allocated for housing, volume housebuilders throw significant resources at forcing the hand of local authorities by repeated appeals on particular sites and by detailed submissions at each stage of local plan preparation, knowing that inspectors at planning inquiries (with an eye on government guidance) will, in many cases, support them. One such aggressive land promoter has hit the headlines. Gladman Land is a Cheshire-based company of land promoters established in 1995. In 2014, it was reported that it was pursuing over 100 greenfield sites on the edges of towns and cities, promising farmers 50 or 60 times the value of their agricultural land if they allow Gladmans to seek planning permission for housing on their sites. Gladman then presses local authorities for planning consents, going to planning appeal after planning appeal if they are rebuffed, arguing that local authorities have not allocated enough land for housing in their local plans (Spencer and Taylor, 2014).

So much land is now under the control of the major builders and land promoters that governments and local authorities are under severe pressure to give them what they want, particularly if crude housing targets remain a government priority. In 2019, a government housing minister suggested that there should be 5 million plots of land available at any one time in the planning system – a massive increase in land allocation for the development industry and a vast potential windfall for landowners.

The result is that, for many years, local authorities have been permanently on the back foot over new development, as described in Ball's (1983) analysis of housebuilders in the 1980s. That was the picture nearly 40 years ago. However, apparently, the government takes the view that local authorities are not enough on the back foot. Post-2012, local authorities are under constant pressure to meet government housing targets and are required to identify a 'deliverable' five-year housing land supply in their districts. This measure effectively gets local authorities to do the housebuilders' jobs for them by identifying potential housing development land. It has had a huge impact on local authority planning decisions and is a great boost to landowners. Not only do local authorities have to scout around for housing sites for fear of government retribution if they do not have a large housing land supply in their local plans, but it has created a loophole around the word 'deliverable'. Since the only people who can say whether a site is deliverable are the people who own it, the local authority is unable to be definitive about whether their five-year land supply is 'deliverable'. The loophole works this way: if a proposed housing scheme has been refused because it is not on the local authority list of five-year supply of housing sites, developers argue that some sites on the list are not truly 'deliverable', whereas (of course) their scheme is and should thus be allowed as an additional site in local authority five-year housing supply plans. This blatantly circular argument has been remarkably successful with inspectors at planning appeals and inquiries.

There is deep unease in the planning profession and anger in communities about government land supply policies, and the land acquisition strategies of developers and landowners – an anger that erupts particularly in times of severe housing shortage. Are developers deliberately buying up land and banking it in order to keep up prices with the hope of making a speculative killing at the right time? Are they rigging the land market? The accusation that land banking is deliberately bidding up prices and perpetuating housing shortages has been an explosive issue in the politics of the housing crisis for a long time. Several high-profile studies have taken place. Adams and Leishman (2008) undertook a study for the government which showed conclusively that developers routinely drip-feed new housing units onto the market in order to keep up prices.

The 2007 *Callcutt review of house building delivery* was tasked with assessing whether the industry had a case to answer. Callcutt himself was formerly the CEO of Crest Nicholson, a major housebuilder from 1991 to 2005, and was perhaps not the ideal person to answer this question objectively. It was no surprise, therefore, that although faced with thousands of unimplemented planning permissions and studies of slow build-out rates, his committee concluded that 'there was no evidence that house builders were holding onto land longer than they need …. Government should take no general measures to force more rapid build out of land banks with implementable planning permissions' (Callcutt, 2007: 35).

Ten years later, in the 2012–18 property boom, the government again responded to public concern about land banking and slow build-out rates. It asked Sir Oliver Letwin, a Conservative MP, to lead a task force to examine why so many planning permissions were not implemented (Letwin, 2018). This review met the same fate at Callcutt. First, the review focused only on sites of 1,500 units, thus ignoring the large number of small- and medium-sized sites. Then, it took as its starting position that any remedial action by the government should not negatively affect land values, house prices or the profits of the housebuilders. Third, it decided that questions of housing tenure, or affordability in new development, were not within its remit. The review acknowledged that build-out rates on large sites owned by the housebuilders were slow but explained this away by saying that developers were responding rationally to local 'absorption rates'. The task force reached the inevitable conclusion that no far-reaching changes in the land delivery system should take place. It completely failed to acknowledge that there is a purpose behind land banking and 'drip-feeding' housing into the market. That purpose is to maintain the price level of developers' new homes. In fact, it is precisely the concept of 'absorption rates' that is the problem. The Letwin recommendations were merely that there should be more 'diversity' of providers on large sites, which is not a bad thing, but, once again, an insider's review of land banking decided that no serious action on land banking should be taken by the government.

Similar bland conclusions have come from investigations into allegations of housebuilder cartels. Here, the suspicion is that housebuilders, in collusion with landowners, operate in local or regional housing markets as an organised group with the aim of maintaining prices and restricting competition. They release sites or distribute development in a controlled way among themselves in order to ensure that price levels are maintained. The Office of Fair Trading (OFT) was asked to look into this in 2008. It identified intense price competition between housebuilders but concluded that the housebuilders had little influence over the general level of prices because, in their view, prices of newbuild tend to be set by the price of the existing stock of housing. The OFT opined that housebuilders were not involved in land hoarding, concluding:

> Having a stock of land helps a homebuilder cope with fluctuations in the housing market and also helps to reduce its exposure to risk resulting from the planning system. We have not found any evidence that homebuilders have the ability to anti-competitively hoard land or own a large amount of land with planning permission on which they have not started to build. Apart from the homebuilding firms, the available information suggests that the largest 'landbank' may be that held by the public sector. (OFT, 2008: 6)

The OFT report was over ten years ago at the onset of the 2008 housing market crash. The last thing that the government wanted at that time was to add fuel to the fire of the property crash by suggesting that there was a rigged market. Since then, things have moved on and housing shortages are worse than ever. There has been another property boom and a very significant consolidation within the sector, with the largest builders having much greater economic power and control over land supplies. At the same time, the finance sector and investors are able to put considerably more pressure on margins, share price and turnover. Given the scale of their landownership and the continuing shortage of new homes, as well as the sky-high profits of the big builders in the recent boom, it is important to once again examine whether there are anti-competitive practices in operation. In a passage considering the consolidation process in the sector, the OFT concluded that 'We do not consider that this amounts to a competition problem although, as with all trends for increasing concentration, it would be prudent that this trend be kept under review' (OFT, 2008: 63). Maybe now is the time for this review.

In 2018, a survey by the Competition and Markets Authority found that over 40 per cent of all firms surveyed (not just property firms) thought that price fixing was legal, and that almost half of firms thought that it was legal to discuss prices with competing bidders. Of significance for housing is that some of the sectors listed as 'most vulnerable to cartels' were construction, estate agents and property management. In other words, in several parts of the country, the property sector is potentially involved in price fixing (Chapman, 2018).

Naturally, the housebuilder response to all of this is that there is no competition problem: all developers are competing with each other and no sane developer would hold land off the market because it is too costly to do so, nor would they fix prices. They agree with Callcutt that it is not the housebuilders that are the problem. They claim that the real villain is the public sector, which, according to them, bears the most responsibility for sites not coming forward for development. They assert that local authorities are holding up development by not allocating enough land in their local plans, are too slow and bureaucratic in updating plans and processing planning applications, and, in many cases, are anti-development. The developers are ready to build but local authorities and the government are not, they say. Even after the government's admission of a 'broken housing market', a survey of the property industry by the Knight Frank agency in 2018 found that the biggest barrier to housing was – guess what – town planning (Knight Frank, 2018). No sign here of any self-reflection or willingness to change.

A further complaint of the sector is that the government and local authorities are holding onto public land that should be sold off for development. It is not the developers and landowners who are the hoarders, but the government. They urge the government to force public land onto the market, claiming that if this happens, more housing will be built and prices miraculously will fall. The Coalition government, responding with enthusiasm to these demands, announced a 'Public Land for Housing Programme 2015–2020'. The top five government landowning departments agreed a contribution towards the public land target of selling off enough land for 160,000 additional homes by the end of March 2020. The agreed contributions were (in housing units): the Ministry of Defence (MoD) = 55,000; the Department for Transport (DfT) = 38,000; the Ministry of Housing, Communities and Local Government/Homes England (MHCLG/HE) = 36,000; the Department of Health and Social Care (DHSC) = 26,000; and the Ministry of Justice (MoJ) = 5,000.

The problem was that much of this land was not, in fact, ready for development; some was still in operational use or in unsuitable sites and not realistically capable of development for housing. In any case, the sale of public land is controversial. For example, is all National Health Service (NHS) land in the disposal register really not needed by the NHS, including, for example, for housing its own staff? What of land held by the MoJ – what exactly are we talking about here: prisons, magistrate courts? Are all these really surplus sites or is this about cuts to services? The ever-present danger is that a public land fire sale is politically expedient – selling off the crown jewels, thus preventing future governments and communities from taking a closer look at the need for these sites and buildings.

Moreover, research by the New Economics Foundation tracking what happened to the land identified in the disposal register found that by 2017, only 9 per cent of the target had been met, and of those completed, only 7 per cent were social rented. What is more, 'in some cases development solely comprises luxury properties' (Wheatley, 2019) – so much for the privatisation of public land helping to solve the housing crisis. As Christophers (2018) concludes in his recent book on public land, the selling of public land is more about ideology than sensible land management.

Grants and subsidies

Returning to the politically sensitive part of the housebuilders' business model, public grants and subsidies are one of the most important elements of the model. They significantly underpin profit margins. The property industry lobbies for six kinds of subsidies:

- tax relief/tax planning on profits from land and property sales and new development;
- subsidies for mortgages, of which the most important is currently Help to Buy;
- grants and loans for infrastructure mainly from Homes England
- grants from European Union structural funds;
- grants from the government for affordable housing and Build to Rent;
- special grants from city deals and enterprise zone allowances.

The total value of these subsidies each year is extraordinary. The Chartered Institute for Housing (CIH, 2018) estimated that of the total £53 billion in government housing investment in 2017, 79 per cent went in direct subsidies to the private sector in that year alone.

The Help to Buy scheme mentioned earlier in this chapter is one of the biggest subsidies to housebuilders ever seen in this country. It is worth looking at in some detail. It is a government mortgage guarantee for homeowners targeted at first-time buyers. Buyers put down a 5 per cent deposit on a new home, take a 40 per cent government loan and get a mortgage for the 55 per cent balance. Thus, if a buyer wants to spend £250,000 on a new home, this would mean finding a deposit of £12,500, taking a government loan of £100,000 and getting a mortgage of £137,500. Between 2013 and 2018, 170,000 homebuyers used Help to Buy. The housebuilders say that this subsidy has increased the supply of new homes that they build by 74 per cent. Unsurprisingly, in a statement in September 2018, the executive chairman of the HBF, Stewart Baseley, announced:

> It is quite clear that the Help to Buy system has been an unmitigated success and has delivered handsomely on its objectives. It has enabled hundreds of thousands of people to realise their dream of owning a home and the vast majority of first time buyers are on average incomes. It has led to an unprecedented increase in housebuilding activity. (Adams, 2018)

In effect, Help to Buy has kept up house prices and enabled housebuilders and their backers to ensure massive profits over the last few years. However, because Help to Buy is eligible for homes priced up to the astonishingly high level of £600,000, much of the subsidy has gone to people who earn well above average incomes. Take an example from the *Evening Standard*'s 'First time buyers supplement' of 26 July 2018: a one-bedroom flat is listed for sale on Chiswick High Road priced at £585,000; this could be bought with a 5 per cent deposit of £29,250, a 45 per cent Help to Buy loan of £234,000 and a 55 per cent mortgage of £323,000. Many similar Help to Buy adverts are listed in this and other supplements. In this circumstance, to what extent does Help to Buy tackle the housing crisis? Is it mainly a bung to housebuilders, landowners and the wealthy? Such is the controversy over Help to Buy that many suggest it should be discontinued, but this is not likely to happen any time soon – the government cannot get off its addiction to subsidising the housebuilders, and the housebuilders are lobbying strongly for it to continue indefinitely.

A test case involves Persimmon Homes, number three in the top ten. Even Conservative newspapers have expressed outrage at the levels of profit taken by housebuilders using Help to Buy. *The Times* carried the following banner front-page headline on 23 February 2019: 'Help to Buy house giant faces loss of contract' (Clarence-Smith et al, 2019). The housing minister at the time threatened to review the participation of Persimmon in future rounds of Help to Buy because the company had made huge profits out of the scheme. The chief executive had taken a £85 million bonus 'despite the company being embroiled in unfair leases and criticised for the quality of some of their homes' (Clarence-Smith et al, 2019) . A devastating investigation of newbuild Persimmon homes was aired by Channel 4's *Dispatches* programme in July 2019. It found a catalogue of expensive defects, yet in spite of this risk to home buyers Persimmon policy does not allow prospective buyers to survey their homes before they are purchased. Persimmon refused to appear on the programme to defend its policies and practices. It remains to be seen whether any real action – beyond exhortation – will be taken by the government. Given its usual form when responding to this sort of revelation, no action is likely. More importantly, this scandal will not stop Help to Buy being extended past its original end date of 2021.

Homes England describes itself as the government's 'housing accelerator'. Much of what it does is aimed at helping out the private housebuilding sector. It operates a £4 billion Homes Building Fund, which is a loan scheme in partnership with Barclays Bank aimed exclusively at private developers. Homes England scrapped (recklessly) its own affordable housing grant scheme, which had run from 2015 to 2018, replacing it with a grant scheme for shared ownership only.

A paltry £163 million up to 2021 was allocated for community housing schemes.

An example of Homes England in action is given in the case studies section of this book. Developers and investors (most of them immensely rich) have been able to extract large sums of subsidy from the government, aided by local authorities who are desperate to get development going on their own land. The developers and investors ask for money for 'infrastructure', which sounds innocuous. The government readily obliges but there is little interrogation of the structure and profits of these companies. For example, do they really need this level of subsidy? How do they benefit from the increase in the value of their land? Nor are there conditions attached about affordability, rent levels or the design of the completed development. Public accountability is down to local authority partners, who often lack the skills or authority to impose strict conditions, and are themselves often restricted by commercial confidentiality agreements with Homes England and development partners.

Conclusion

The commercial housebuilding sector has expanded and consolidated over the last 25 years, with big companies now dominating, and increasingly integrated with the finance and investment sector. As a result, the major companies have gained significantly more political power and influence, making it more difficult for the government, local authorities or communities to tackle the housing crisis. In fact, this growing power and influence has made the crisis worse.

The objective of the housebuilder–finance business is to profit from increasing the value of the land they own and trade, and the houses they sell. This imperative has huge repercussions for the housing crisis because it places the priority of the market on increasing values rather than on meeting housing need. Increasing values means higher prices, lower affordability and fewer housing providers (because smaller or not-for-profit housebuilders cannot afford to buy land). The housebuilders have become highly skilled at protecting their successful business model by accumulating large land banks at the right time and place so that their value increases with the prospect of new development, and by drip-feeding new homes onto the market to keep up prices.

Yet, it is also apparent that the business model cannot rely on the market alone; at heart, it is a political model. It needs local authorities and government to allocate land for housing in order to feed their land banks, and it requires the government to provide a steady stream of grants and subsidies to secure their profit margins and remove their risks. Thus, the government gives grants to developers for land remediation and infrastructure estimated at £12 billion a year to reduce their costs, and helps homebuyers with mortgage payments – all of which maintains price levels for the housebuilders. This support is particularly forthcoming after a slump in the property market because governments are so dependent on the market to build new homes. Since 2010, governments have created a situation where they have no other way of meeting their own targets for new homes than by underpinning extensive housebuilder land banking.

Successive governments have created a bind of their own making. They have created no independent mechanism to solve the housing crisis because they have all but stopped council housebuilding by local authorities, they have sold off public land and they insist on continuing with Right to Buy, which depletes the social housing stock. They have sunk deeper and deeper into the grip of the property development market, without the means to remedy the housing crisis. The government can only create a pretence that it is doing something to tackle it by announcing that it is in partnership with the development sector; however, it knows full well that this will not make a dent on affordability or on housing need.

The integration of land and the volume housebuilding sector with City investment markets reinforces political and financial blockages to reform because of their profit-oriented and risk-averse strategies. It Chapter 4,we take a closer look at where the property market is placed within the national economy and the role of the investment sector in the housing crisis.

4

Financing housing investment

In Chapter 3, we looked at the housebuilding business from the point of view of the volume housebuilders. Now, we need to look behind the builders and the developers at the financial institutions and investors that fund them and set the conditions under which they operate. The structure and practices of property investor groups have immense influence over the availability and cost of housing in the UK and, as I shall argue, are a principal barrier to resolving the housing crisis. This chapter therefore charts the growth of the investors and finance houses behind the UK land and property market, and examines the nature of their power and vested interests.

It is important to emphasise, as many others have done, that the UK economy is heavily dependent on land and property, and on the housing market in particular. Ryan Collins et al (2017: 160) say in their book on the economics of land and housing: 'The wider economy remains intimately linked to the value of land and property both through the provision of liquidity to SMEs [small- and medium-sized enterprises] via commercial real estate as well as the collateral and wealth channels that play a key role in supporting consumption'. Housing, in particular, is now a principal underpinning of the banking system and of corporate borrowing. This is why 'successive governments have sought to increase or at least maintain both house prices and home ownership levels' (Ryan-Collins et al, 2017: 147). The housing market is thus used by the government to regulate economic growth and stimulate domestic consumption.

The opportunity for windfall profits made on land has a particular attraction to speculators. Their activities have led to bouts of either over- or under-building and price fluctuations, which make the economy particularly susceptible to property booms and busts. Larry Elliot, economics correspondent for *The Guardian*, summed up the unstable nature of the UK economic model as follows: 'An economic model that cannot function without repeated injections of property inflation is built on shaky foundations' (Elliott, 2018).

The UK economy is not the only economy that suffers in this way. Spain, Ireland and Greece are other contenders whose economies have been highly vulnerable to property booms and busts. In his memoir of the Eurozone crisis in 2013/14, Yanis Varoufakis describes how speculators poured their money into property in Greece. His comment that 'real estate is the natural ally of any financial bubble' (Varoufakis, 2017: 75) applies equally to the UK.

A large chunk of the money poured into property in the UK is speculative money, both from within the UK and internationally, looking for safe houses for profits, or for opportunities for short-term gain. Shrubsole (2019: 121) describes the large investments in recent years by the ultra-rich in properties in London and the South East, not forgetting the purchase of Scottish grouse moors. Many of the properties are held in trusts and are registered offshore. Being ultra-rich is not enough; tax avoidance is necessary as well.

Although this sounds like the Wild West, none of this could happen without the involvement of the government and approval of the Treasury. Directly or indirectly, the UK property and housing markets have been primed by the government on many occasions over the past 30 years. We have seen how it has funded dozens of stimulus schemes such as Help to Buy and Homes England funding, and when George Osborne was Chancellor in the mid-2010s, the government also deliberately attracted speculative global funds into the UK, rewarding inward investors for doing so with promises of resident status and cuts in corporation tax. Osborne's purpose was to increase the government's tax take from the rich but the result was an increase in property prices in London to unsustainable levels for everyone else.

Similarly, the huge injection of quantitative easing (QE) between 2009 and 2012, and again in 2016, had the same effect: pushing up property asset prices. The Bank of England made asset purchases of £475 billion from financial institutions. The purpose was to reflate the economy by putting more institutional money into circulation after the 2008 financial crash and the recession that followed, but the effect was to increase lending to property, pushing up the price of property assets, which contributed to the property boom and crisis of affordability from 2012 onwards.

QE activity was aimed mainly at the commercial real estate sector, but ordinary homeowners were caught up in the house price spiral as well. Homeowner house prices have assumed extraordinary importance in the UK economy and in consumer behaviour over the past 40 years. In his analysis of land and housing in the UK, Michael Edwards (2015: 8) emphasises the exceptional role of asset values in the UK economy and summarises the impact on housing in the following way: 'The British version of the housing problem relates to the UK's strong focus on property as assets and the ownership and market practices which have evolved in land and property markets.' His research shows a sharp rise in the value of 'tangible assets' since the 1980s, of which property is one of the most important categories. Between 1988 and 2009, the total value of residential property rose by four times, reflecting the national preoccupation with housing values for both homeowners and policymakers, and the scale of the credit boom that made this possible.

Asset price inflation has led to billions of pounds of investment being diverted from productive or community investment into commercial and housing real estate by banks, pension funds, insurance companies, sovereign wealth funds and other investment funds. Up until the 1980s, pension funds typically held 20 per cent of their total investment in property, and although their investment in property subsequently fell back due to fears of property booms and busts, the total amount of institutional funding of all types in property is astronomical. A survey of 48 major UK investors in 2018 showed that they controlled total assets of £8.2 trillion, of which £246 billion was in real estate (Portlock, 2018).

The scramble for land

A further source of immense power in the property market is landownership. For many years, large-scale landownership has been heavily concentrated in the hands of landed estates, the Crown, big corporations and the government, as charted by Massey and Catalano (1978), Cahill (2001), Wightman (1996) and, most recently, Shrubsole (2019). Two things have happened to the nature of this landownership in recent years. First, traditional landowners are no longer sitting on their land assets with no apparent urgency to develop them. In his book on major landowners in the UK, Richard Norton-Taylor (1982) describes how this began in the late 1970s 'when monetary considerations replaced inheritance, residence and social responsibility'. The traditional landowning class is now actively involved in strategies to increase the value of their land assets by sale, development or more intensive use. Volume housebuilders are thus finding many more traditional landowners willing to take out residential development options.

The second change is the one charted brilliantly by Saskia Sassen (2014). She identified a major shift in global landownership beginning in 2006, when there was a sharp increase in foreign acquisitions of rural land for food crops, leading to the expulsion and disempowerment of rural communities (Sassen, 2015). Since the 2008 financial crash and the recession, she has identified a further shift: a global scramble for urban land for security and as a long-term investment. She sees this as a step change: an out of the ordinary increase in strategic land acquisitions, signalling a new alignment of power in land and housing markets. She calculates that in 100 global cities, foreign buyers are accumulating 1 trillion US dollars of investment in land and property every year. This includes vacant and derelict industrial land that is relatively cheap but, significantly (with the right kind of pressure on the government), has potential for up-market housing. Governments desperate for inward investment, including the UK, are backing this process, often with tax incentives and public funding for land reclamation and transport infrastructure. Later in this book, we single out an example of this globalised land grab in the development of the Greenwich Peninsula, a former gas board site in South London.

The UK has opened its doors to overseas property investors in a big way, offering generous tax breaks for overseas investors. Lizieri et al (2011) reported that foreign ownership in the City of London rose from 6 per cent in 1972, to 10 per cent in 1985, and to 50 per cent in 2011. In a paper for the Smith Institute in 2012, Heywood estimated that 60 per cent of all new homes in central London were being bought by overseas investors (Heywood, 2012). According to a survey of international investment in London housing, between 2014 and 2016, investors from Hong Kong and Singapore snapped up 3,600 of London's 28,000 newly built homes during that period. Interestingly, about half of those bought were priced for first-time buyers – between £200,000 and £500,000 – but will now be sold on to other parts of the market (Booth, 2017). In 2018, it was suggested that international buyers plan to invest a further £40 billion in London.

In 2017, the British Broadcasting Corporation (BBC) *McMafia* drama series touched on the concern that criminal activities often have a close association with property investment, especially in London. This is not new: £10 million of the proceeds of the 1983 Brink's-Mat robbery were invested in luxury apartment blocks in London Docklands in the 1980s. The role of property as 'safe houses' (literally) for wealth funds, whether legitimate or criminal, creates a tangle of powerful interests that makes reform much more difficult.

Rocketing land prices

Due to the corporate scramble for land and for the intensification of development, land prices have rocketed over the last 20 years. The value of land in the UK has recently been put at £10 trillion representing 51 per cent of UK net worth, with data showing that it is rising at a rate of £450 billion a year (Inman, 2018). Whereas the value of land represented 20 per cent of the price of a house 30 years ago, it is now closer to 75 per cent in some areas (ITV, 2018). Under these circumstances, large- and medium-sized landowners have immense power over the value, location and quality of housing development in the country. There is fiercer competition for sites and, consequently, developers are paying more for land, pushing up house prices, increasing densities and driving out less wealthy housing providers. Developers are using this as a reason (the merits of which we examine later) for reducing the level of planning gain and community benefit required by local planning authorities.

Mortgage dependency

All of this finds its way into the price of mortgages, with mortgages a larger and larger part of the UK economy. Mortgage lending via banks and building societies is mainly for homeownership, Buy to Let or small-scale property development. In 2013, it was reported that UK household debt was the highest in the world, at a whopping £1.8 trillion. It grew by 7 per cent in the five years from 2012 to 2017, largely due to mortgage lending, which reached the highest level since the days before the financial crash in 2008. According to Mortgage Strategy, a gross total of £257 billion was loaned in 2017, up 4 per cent on 2016. The largest share of loans was made by Lloyds, RBS, Santander and Barclays, with Nationwide the only mutual mortgage company in the top five.[1]

The mortgage market is highly dependent upon interest rates and mortgage relief schemes such as Help to Buy (as we saw in Chapter 3), and for this reason, the UK housing market is closely monitored by the government and the Bank of England at the highest level. Yet, maintaining stability in mortgage lending and house prices is almost impossible in the speculative world of UK housing markets. There are so many financial interests that benefit from ever-rising prices that regulators can be completely blindsided – as happened in the 2008 financial crash, which the government claimed not to see coming, as discussed further in Chapter 7.

Although residential mortgage lending is not primarily a corporate investment sector, it can be securitised, as we saw in the sub-prime housing scandal, particularly in the US, which led to the financial crash of 2008. During this calamity, mortgages were packaged up to enable investors to speculate on property prices. The collapse of this market had a massive knock-on effect on the global financial system and the UK economy – and without proper regulation, it could happen again.

Housing becomes commercial property

The commercial property investment sector operates in a different way. Investors focus on returns from individual development schemes, whether on a short-term or long-term basis. Their aim is to maximise rental income (yields) and capital gains over the long term from investment properties that they have either bought or leased. They also trade in property company shareholdings. Real Estate Investment Trusts (REITs), whose attraction is that they carry tax relief from investing in property company shares, have grown rapidly over the last 15 years in the UK (Baum, 2015: 162). After the regulations establishing REITs in the UK in 2006, several UK property companies have converted to REITs, including household names such as Land Securities, Hammerson and British Land. Thus, we have the bizarre situation that some of the biggest developers and speculators in land and property in the UK are, in fact, 'trusts' – expertly reducing their tax liabilities because they are presenting themselves as something other than real estate investors.

Banks and finance houses began funding commercial property development in the 1960s, focusing on offices in prime locations in major cities, though mainly in London. Now, their portfolios have broadened to include industrial, retail, leisure and, more recently, residential property and land (BPF, 2013). Detailed work on UK property cycles undertaken by Barras noted that it was from the late 1980s that the property market went global, with the 'ever closer integration of capital and real estate markets' (Barras, 2009: 75); in this period, 'investor involvement in property development rose markedly contributing to the increased amplitude and volatility of booms and slumps' (Barras, 2009: 71). Thus, globalisation and investor involvement sparked by City deregulation in the 1980s has made managing the property industry and the housing crisis a great deal more difficult.

The integration of City finance with real estate has had a marked effect on the structure of property investment. Within the property investment industry, there has been a traditional divide between commercial real estate (office, industrial, retail and leisure) and residential. For many years, these sectors were separate as far as investors were concerned because housing provided few opportunities for reliable long-term income growth. It was regarded as more risky than commercial development, and it involved the additional costs of managing residential property.

However, in recent years, the two wings of property development and investment – commercial real estate and residential – have come together, being increasingly integrated within individual companies and investor groups. Large mixed development schemes in city centres, combining private residential units with offices or retail, attract investors in both residential and offices. Driving this forward is the upsurge in Build to Rent. Build to Rent is very different from the private lettings businesses operated by thousands of small landlords. It is about building or purchasing high-quality private housing developments that can guarantee long-term rental growth, with housing management outsourced to property management companies. In other words, it is a standard commercial property investment applied to housing.

The government has become enthusiastic about Build to Rent as one means of attracting institutional capital into housebuilding. Compared with other types of housing, it attracts funding from pension funds, banks and insurance funds. There was a surprising announcement at the end of 2018 that Legal and General (L&G), one of the largest insurance companies, was to set up an 'affordable housing' subsidiary. Yet, do not be misled by labels. The L&G version of affordable housing is the higher-rent end of the Built to Rent sector; as such, it is a good fit with housing as an investment.

The consequence of the integration of landownership and residential development in the wider investment market is that the housebuilding sector is no longer on the margins of the City, but deep inside it. For decades, the sector has been regarded as somewhat cavalier, not fully integrated into the mainstream of UK business. However, this has changed. As we have seen, housebuilding companies have consolidated into major corporate organisations, and as the sector has become more successful, they have attracted direct investor interest from both the UK and overseas. The increasing integration of investors, property companies and landowners – with large construction companies also in the mix – creates a formidable political and economic lobby. This presents a completely new challenge for those seeking the reform of the housing market or the resolution of the housing crisis. It is not just a question of tackling the housebuilders or landowners, but one of tackling a deeper and wider range of City financial interests.

Prices and politics

The City takeover of the housing market raises fundamental questions about the merits of high or low property prices. While renters and those wishing to buy want lower prices, a constant rise in land and property prices is the imperative of the investment sector. Rising prices have traditionally been the goal of investors to a greater or less extent, but it is now a more comprehensive and systematised imperative, locking housing into City financial markets, with much less scope for individual variation or social conscience. Thus, while most of the country agonises about exorbitant housing prices and the lack of affordability, the investment and development sectors welcome property price inflation and, indeed, depend upon it. They require steadily increasing prices and income growth from land and property for their business model to work and are immune to concerns about the lack of affordability – unless the government requires them to be so. Property investors need the housing crisis to continue in order to ensure the flow of profits into their business. The gulf between the world of property investment and the reality of tackling the housing crisis could not be wider.

This underlying conflict comes into even sharper focus when we observe the politics of property taxation. Taxation is fundamental to all property development because it can make the difference between a windfall gain and a small profit. One expert in the field told the author that tax was the most important policy issue for real estate and development, well ahead of issues of planning or housing legislation. Levels of tax for capital gains, investment income, stamp duty and business rates are the critical politics of land and property for investors and developers. This is why lobbying on property taxes is such a massive industry and why REITs have become so common in the UK and elsewhere. Lowering or avoiding capital gains tax is a key objective for landowners. Financial advisers for landowners, developers and property investors will search out the most favourable regimes to locate their business or lodge their accounts: 'Companies set up in the Channel Islands for example, can sell property free of all UK capital gains tax. For this reason and others, the UK is seen to some extent as a tax haven for international investors' (Baum, 2015: 262).

Whenever land and property taxes are reduced or waived such that investors capture more of the land value from development, less value is available for society and the community. The argument that these investors include pension funds 'in which we all have a stake' seems hollow when the very communities that created the value are struggling to be properly housed or make ends meet. One has to ask how much property pension fund investment or REITs funding is finding its way into helping Britain's poorer communities – I would suggest none.

Conclusion

The UK economy is underpinned to an exceptional degree by property values and property speculation, making it highly vulnerable to booms and slumps, and misdirected investment. Governments are locked into this structure and actively support it with tax breaks and light regulation, having become dependent upon it for tax revenues and political support.

Thus, backstage in the housing crisis, City finance and overseas investors are working to ensure that government tax and regulation regimes for property, land and housing development do not hinder their planned trajectory of growth in values and prices. Policies that reduce land and property values, whether taxes, demands for more planning gain or greater environmental or building regulations, threaten investor returns. Under these circumstances, lobbying the government to limit land and property market regulation and taxation is a top priority for City finance, whatever the consequences for the wider economy, society or the environment – and they usually succeed.

Each type of real estate investment (banks, pension funds, hedge funds and so on) has its own channel of influence and political leverage over housing policy but, together, they are able to exert pressure on the government over the regulation of and subsidies to land and housing development. Whether they work in concert or share common policy objectives to influence particular policies we shall examine in Chapter 5.

5

The property lobby

Such is the scale of economic and political power in UK land and property that one wonders if it needs an organised political lobby to protect its interests. Its seems as if the balance of power has swung so much in favour of land and property that it is baked into the UK economy and institutions, and that supporting it is the 'natural thing to do' as far as governments are concerned. Perhaps its power is so great that no one dares tackle it. Yet, in fact, the property lobby is one of the best organised, well-funded and well-connected political lobbies in the UK.

Land and property power is always afraid of having its dominance reduced; it is terrified of any state or community interference that will reduce its sway. There are many property interests to protect and enhance; all want to keep the pressure on the government, irrespective of the overall property tilt of the economy. The property lobby ranges from organisations supporting developers and landowners, such as the HBF and the Country Land and Business Association (CLA; formerly known as the Country Landowners Association), to professional property associations, such as the RICS. The lobby also includes informal parliamentary groups and countless routine meetings between politicians, civil servants, developers and landowners. In turn, they are closely connected to right-of-centre think tanks such as the Centre for Policy Studies and the Institute for Economic Affairs. The aim of this chapter is to identify the main players in the property lobby and their campaign strategies. How much influence do they have and what are their successes and failures?

Political lobbying is a professionalised and well organised business – it is not left to chance or to personal contacts. Property companies and landowner groups routinely employ lobbyists to make their case to the government on issues affecting their own business. In addition, they join the main property industry lobby groups to give their support and funding to political campaigns on wider land and planning policy. Research published by the Bureau of Investigative Journalists identified a large number of prominent household names in the commercial property sector who make extensive use of professional political consultants to advocate their case on specific issues to the government (Mathiason et al, 2012).

The property lobby organisations representing housebuilders, bankers, landowners and surveyors do not like to be described as lobby groups. They prefer the terms 'trade associations', 'membership organisations' or 'professional bodies', thus presenting themselves as benign and non-political. However, political lobbying is what they do, and in their list of principal objectives, parliamentary activity is always high up on the list. Communication with the government and the media, submissions to government consultations, and invitations to government ministers to speak at their events are central to their function. They operate at both Whitehall and usually at the local level as well. The HBF, for example, makes detailed submissions to local plan inquiries and examinations to advocate land allocations, housing targets, planning gain policies and planning standards. In addition to its day job of setting and monitoring professional standards in surveying and valuation, the RICS regularly produces press releases, and its policy committees advocate a wide range of interventions. The CLA places 'influence' (lobbying and campaigning) at the top of its organisational objectives.

Although national organisations, the property lobby organisations have a traditional geography. Their headquarters are located in Central London close to government departments and Parliament, and their memberships and client base are strongly centred on land and property in London and across the South East of England. Their lobbying activities are focused largely (though not exclusively) on Whitehall policymakers.

Publications and research are a key part of lobbying strategies. Most property groups produce their own journals and magazines, for example, *Housebuilder* from the HBF, the *Land and Business Magazine* from the CLA or the *Land Journal* from the RICS. These journals present the viewpoint of their organisations on policy, give their spin on data on housing statistics, construction activity and development projects, and give feedback on their industry and social events. Several organisations, such as the RICS, the British Property Federation (BPF) and the CLA, employ their own researchers and fund research from universities and other external bodies.

There are other property trade magazines that, although not produced by the main property lobby groups, rely on advertising from the property sector, as well as reporting on individual property development schemes and government announcements. They include journals like *Building*, *Estates Gazette*, *Building Design*, *Architects Journal* and many others covering built environment businesses and professionals.

The Country Land and Business Association (CLA)

The largest landowner lobby group is the CLA. Situated in Belgrave Square in London, the CLA describes itself on its web site as 'the established voice for landowning rural businesses in Government'.[1] This description is somewhat of an understatement since the CLA, with 33,000 members, is the voice of many of the largest private landowning groups and institutions in the country, in other words, rather more than 'rural businesses'. Its previous name, the 'Country Landowners Association', is a more accurate description of its role.

The CLA was founded in 1907 at a meeting of wealthy landowners and Conservative MPs at the Carlton Club in response to the Liberal government election in 1906. That government had pledged to tackle the problem of unequal landownership and the poor treatment of agricultural workers. The biographer of the CLA, Charles Clover has described the CLA response in this way: 'The full fronted attack on private property was seldom as fierce as after the Liberal landslide of 1906. The followers of Lloyd George openly favoured land nationalisation, following penal taxation. The first was seen off, but not the latter' (Clover, 2017).

According to Clover, 60 per cent of the members of the CLA are small landowners and farmers owning less than 100 acres, and only 4 per cent are landowners owning over 1,000 acres. The main preoccupation of the CLA has been to support farmers and landowners and to protect them from legislation that may limit their activities (which includes the right to build on their land). Despite its protests over many years at state intervention in landownership, the CLA has been forced to accept that the public has a right to increased access to the countryside (though, as Shrubsole [2019] notes, this right is strictly limited), and that planning legislation and environmental legislation are necessary. However, the CLA's bottom line is to resist the public ownership or taxation of land. As Charles Clover (2017) again states: 'The CLA has a pre-disposition towards classical Anglo-American free enterprise.'

The CLA claims that its members own and manage around half the rural land in England and Wales. In its own words: 'This puts the CLA in an unrivalled position to influence, develop and debate policy that will achieve real change. We work with policy makers and politicians at every level to raise awareness of the issues affecting our members' businesses'.[2] The CLA has six regional offices that lobby on local rural issues, working with the devolved governments, while its public affairs team influences policy at the national and European levels. Its website says that the CLA:

- maintains a constant dialogue with key decision-makers;
- works as a sector by liaising with stakeholder organisations;
- provides briefings for debates and laying parliamentary questions; and
- makes members' voices heard in relevant government consultations and inquiries.

The CLA pitch to its members is as follows:

> Every day decisions are taken in Whitehall, Cardiff and Brussels that have an impact on you and your ability to manage your land and business effectively ... The CLA makes the case for rural land and business owners at the heart of Government. We meet regularly with UK and Welsh Ministers, MPs and AMs, as well as MEPs and EU Commissioners, and we promote your interests through the media and policy-making groups ... CLA's influence ensures that policy-makers take the best possible account of the needs of rural land, property and business owners, and members benefit from an understanding of the decisions that affect them.[3]

One of the main concerns of the CLA is the regulation of development in rural areas. Its objective is to press the government and local authorities to permit landowners and rural businesses to grow their businesses with minimum restrictions – and be encouraged to do so by agricultural subsidies and other support where possible. Rural industrial and farming businesses want more flexibility over building permissions in rural areas; hence, the CLA makes frequent submissions to the government and to local plan inquiries advocating more flexibility over developing land for housing and industry in rural locations.

More significant to the CLA is its concern about the taxation of land, that is, the fear that the government will take more of the proceeds from trading in land or selling land for development. The CLA is incensed by the public perception that landowners are pocketing windfall sums from the increase in land value (which could be up to 100 times agricultural value) arising from obtaining planning consent for housing on farmland. A press release from the Centre for Progressive Policy and the National Housing Federation (Centre for Progressive Policy, 2018) suggested that landowners were making 'billions' from obtaining planning permissions for housing, and that the government should take action to capture this windfall. The CLA immediately issued a statement strongly denying that billions were made, claiming that the data used in the report exaggerated the amount of profit that could be obtained – they did not deny that windfalls were made, just the amount of the windfall.

Nevertheless, whatever the CLA may wish, the issue of land value capture has risen up the political agenda. When CIL was first announced, the CLA issued a press release stating 'Additional taxes on new development by local authorities serve only to stop growth and stagnate economies' (CLA, 2013). Later, in response to a government consultation in 2017 entitled 'Supporting housing delivery through developer contributions', which merely and quite reasonably proposed that CIL charges to pay for infrastructure for housing might be increased, the CLA responded: 'The consultation proposals appear to remove virtually all incentives for landowners to bring agricultural land forward for development' (CLA, 2018a). This is, of course, a wild overstatement of the risk to landowners from small increases in planning charges when they bring land forward for development in a booming land market. What the CLA really means is: 'Don't reduce the amount of windfall profit we make from selling land for housing, and thank you for giving us another excuse for withholding much-needed land from the market so that it can increase further in value over time.' Again, when a select committee of the House of Commons reported on planning charges and land value capture in September 2018, the CLA made submissions arguing that current mechanisms for land value capture (Section 106 and CIL [CLA, 2018b], as discussed in Chapter 10) were working well and no further measures were needed.

A similar response followed a Labour Party review of planning in 2018, which said that more use should be made of Compulsory Purchase Orders (CPOs) to bring land forward for development and capture more land value for the community. The CLA promptly issued a press statement from their director of policy and advice on 24 September 2018 (CLA, 2018c), saying: 'The current system of capturing land value already has the means to fund infrastructure such as housing. We do not support any changes that would make the process even more complex and adversarial.' It is noteworthy that this most historically combative lobby group should accuse others of being adversarial.

Large landowners have benefitted from the remarkable secrecy that surrounds landownership and land-trading profits in the UK. Cahill (2001) and Shrubsole (2019) have exposed the extensive non-registration and non-disclosure of landed assets in their path-breaking work on Britain's landowners. Moreover, as private companies, individuals and family trusts, many landowners have been able to keep their businesses hidden from public scrutiny. Whether their profits and windfall gains are fully disclosed to Her Majesty's Revenue and Customs (HMRC) we just do not know. We do know from the 'Panama Papers' that many of these landowner groups use offshore trusts to hide their money and their ownerships in tax havens. Even in the age of freedom of information, there is almost no published information on landowner profits from development, either on an annual or project-by-project basis. This compares with the property development sector, which does at least publish its annual profits in its company accounts (though, notably, developers do not publish profits from individual schemes).

The CLA's defence of landowner rights has proved to be extremely effective in development viability assessments, giving credence to landowner opinions on what is a reasonable landowner profit to be made from selling development land. In the absence of published data, or 'industry standards' for landowner profits, existing market prices for land are used as a benchmark as to what is a reasonable land value. Indeed, local authority planners are usually expected to ask local landowners to gauge what is a reasonable price for land (Harman, 2012: 31). This circularity to protect landowner vested interests means that, in essence, almost everybody, including public authorities and developers, are paying inflated market prices for land – prices that are simply windfall gains for landowners who have contributed nothing to create value and, in fact, have made the housing crisis worse by bidding up land prices. Hence, house buyers or renters are paying far more for land than they should just because landowners have a stranglehold on the land market and have the power to protect their own secrecy. The result is that housing is unaffordable.

Whenever there are suggestions by academic researchers or think tanks that land values should be taxed, or that windfall development gains should be subject to higher levels of tax, the landowner lobby has been instrumental in marshalling the press and media against this. Recall the row in 2015 over Labour Party proposals under Ed Miliband that land should be subject to 'use it or lose it', that is, development land should be compulsorily acquired if it had planning permission for housing but was being held off the market by the landowner. This measure was hysterically labelled by the *Daily Mail* and other papers as a 'Stalinist land grab' and a 'garden tax', whereas, in fact, it had nothing to do with the acquisition of private homes or gardens, but was about potential housing development land tied up in developer land banks.

For over a century, big landowners have succeeded beyond their dreams in overthrowing popular proposals for land nationalisation or taxation when they have arisen. They have been supported by right-wing think tanks such as the Centre for Policy Studies and the Institute for Economic Affairs, whose pamphlets and lobbying have been in the vanguard of attacks on public landownership (Christophers, 2018: 138).

Conservative governments (usually comprising a number of wealthy landowners associated with the CLA) have proved to be immensely loyal and protective of landowner interests, acting quickly to overturn legislation that threatens their rights or windfall profits. A land value tax was included in the 1909 Liberal government budget but it was repealed in 1920 before it got off the ground. This was the first major victory for the CLA. In 1951, the Development Charge (part of the 1947 town planning reform) was scrapped by the incoming Conservative government, ironically under the premiership of Winston Churchill, who had been a champion of land value taxation in an earlier time. Further measures by Labour governments in the 1960s and 1970s to capture development gain and reduce land speculation were quickly reversed by incoming Conservative governments (Cullingworth, 1999). Conservative Party loyalty to the landowner class knows no bounds. Some 100 years on from their historic victory against land value taxation in 1920, and despite the acute housing shortage, the landowner lobby is still actively lobbying politicians against touching privately owned development land.

Where the public sector does seek to acquire land by CPO, the property lobby has again stepped in to make this an extremely difficult and expensive process. The Land Compensation Act 1961, brought in by the Conservative government of the time, requires that the price paid for the compulsory purchase of land should be not the existing use value of the land, but the market value of the land, that is, the price it would realise if sold on the open market. Amazingly this legislation is still on the statute book 60 years later. It means that the public are paying for the hope value of land when the purpose of a CPO is to bring forward land for development in the public interest, for example, for transport links, affordable housing, community facilities and open space. Plainly, the cost to the public purse of buying land at these values inhibits the use of CPOs.

The Land Promoters and Developers Federation (LPDF)

The LPDF is a recently formed association, set up in 2018, now with 20 members who are landowners and land promoters. One of its members, and also on its board, is Gladman Land, mentioned earlier in Chapter 3. The LPDF describes itself as a collaboration of the UK's leading land promotion and development businesses. Its aim is to enable the land promotion sector to 'speak with one voice'. It supports the housebuilding sector by providing 'oven-ready' land for planning permission and development. In this activity, it focuses on sites from 30 homes up to 10,000 homes. It is chaired by the CEO of Catesby Estates, a company who operate in Warwickshire specialising in 'the delivery of residential planning consents'.

Much of what the LPDF does is lobbying the government by making submissions on developer contributions, land value capture and CPOs. It lobbies against measures that, according to their web site, will 'dis-incentivise landowners from bringing their land forward for development'.[4] Thus, it is opposed to removing market valuations from CPO compensation or measures for increasing land value capture – existing measures for capturing planning gain are quite enough as far as they are concerned. The LPDF is a small organisation but its existence indicates the pressure piling up on the government to allocate more land for housing and resist concessions on land value capture.

The Royal Institution of Chartered Surveyors (RICS)

Situated in a grand Victorian building immediately opposite the House of Commons in Parliament Square is the 150-year-old RICS. Appropriately, the pillar of UK land surveying and valuation stands across the road from the UK Parliament building. The RICS is a professional body for surveyors and valuers, with status as an accrediting body and champion of professional standards. Yet, it is a lot more than that.

Like other property organisations, the RICS does not like to be described as an industry lobby group. Its royal charter says that it exists to serve the public interest. It is true that it is not an obvious vested interest lobby group like landowners or developers; it operates in a more nuanced way. Yet, it has numerous committees advocating policy on all aspects of land planning and valuation. Its credibility as a professional accrediting body for valuation gives it ready access to government decision-making. For example, it directly advised the government on the NPPF in 2012 and advised the Letwin committee on developer build-out rates. Its advice tends towards one direction: to protect land values and landowner/developer interests. As an RICS official acknowledged to the author: "We are market conscious; value is a default; we speak the language of deliverability." The RICS sees itself as offering "rational methods for entrepreneurial risk taking".

To this end, it defends its own market-oriented property valuation methods which take little account of social or environmental values.

Given that most of its clients (and fees) come from the commercial side of the property market rather than from public or community bodies, its bias is inevitable. The RICS claims to support the objective of sustainable development but this appears to be defined in narrow governmental terms as a presumption in favour of development if it can be shown to be commercially viable. The tilt of the RICS towards market values is best seen in practical terms in day-to-day local government disputes about housing and land development, where RICS valuations push up prices – a process that is hugely damaging to efforts to tackle the housing crisis. This price escalation works because RICS valuations build in current market prices as benchmarks and their clients – landowners and developers – inevitably use them as starting points to move prices ever upwards.

The RICS qualification carries a lot more weight in property disputes and local planning than the RTPI. This is because valuers deal with land value, the money side of locations and the environment, while planners only deal with land use. RICS valuation methods are regarded as the last word on property valuation in the UK. Yet, as explained in Chapter 3, property valuation has many subjective/political elements so that different valuers will come up with different values, particularly on large sites or major developments. Moreover, social and environmental values, which communities are equally concerned about in planning disputes, are almost never taken into account in RICS valuation methodologies. For example, despite the climate crisis, the RICS 'Red Book' revision of global valuation standards in 2017 states that collecting data on sustainability for valuation purposes is not mandatory (RICS, 2017).[5] Nevertheless, the RICS is able to hide these fundamental drawbacks because of its privileged position in the UK land and property sector and especially in Whitehall, where its power and methodologies are never challenged.

In summary, the RICS not only dominates the land and planning marketplace from a professional point of view, but also, by its presence and parliamentary lobbying, maintains the market-oriented bias in the politics of land, housing and planning. It supports a 'managed market' in land and housing, and seeks reforms in that context, rather than advocating interventions that would rebalance the market towards social and environmental outcomes. Although it claims not to support out-and-out property speculation or 'land value extraction', as it has been described, it says that its objective is to maintain an 'equilibrium' in the balance between the property market and planning. One has to ask whether this so-called 'equilibrium' is not, in fact, the current imbalance between the property market and town planning. In other words, it is an equilibrium defined by RICS members, who are the advisers to property investors and financial groups wedded to increasing asset values. The RICS warns against policies that aim to control land or property prices because it says that "People are locked into values; homes are a piggy bank." They seem blind to the fact that the commercial property investors and financial institutions that they advise are also 'locked into values' and it is these investors who exercise influence over national policy on housing development.

The Home Builders Federation (HBF)

The volume housebuilders lobby has become increasingly vocal in land and planning policy over the last 30 years. Housebuilders in England and Wales are represented by the HBF. While there are other sector groupings mainly related to construction, such as the Master Builders, the HBF is by far the most politically active.

There are 330 housebuilder company members in the HBF, including most of the prominent volume builders in the top 20. In addition, it has 2,000 associate members, from consultancies to product suppliers. It has only a few local authority and housing association members or commercial real estate company members (see later on the BPF). The HBF claim that their members represent 80 per cent of all new homes built in England and Wales.

The association was formed in 1939 and became known as the House Builders Federation in 1970. It changed its name to the friendlier 'Home Builders Federation' in 2005. Like the CLA it calls itself a trade organisation but, above all, it is a political lobby. Although a smallish organisation with 20 members of staff and no research department, it carries significant political influence.

The HBF's stated two principal aims are:

- to ensure senior politicians and government officials are aware of the housing issues and challenges that affect HBF members; and
- to work with government officials to ensure that housing policies facilitate housing supply.

Short et al (1986) and Rydin (1993) have charted how the HBF grew to prominence in the 1980s, becoming more aggressive and policy focused. Ball's (1983: 254) housing research in the 1980s led him to conclude that 'there has been sustained political lobbying by housebuilders against existing planning policies'. The HBF had direct influence over drafting government circulars recalibrating the planning system when the Thatcher government came into office in 1979. Short et al (1986) comment that during that time, there was 'a steady increase in the way builder-developer demands have been incorporated in the language and practice of land use planning'. Michael Heseltine was described as 'very amenable to approaches by house-builders' and, of course, as Secretary of State for the Environment, he was able to direct local authorities to allocate land for volume housebuilding in their local plans. That was the 1980s; nowadays, the HBF is even more firmly established, and not just with Conservative governments. As the sector has become more successful and consolidated, it has become the first port of call for politicians and civil servants, particularly when it comes to the consideration of housing targets and land supply. The HBF says that their most effective means of influence is by direct ministerial contact. It sees itself as having influenced the policies of both Labour and Conservative governments.

The key strategic issues for the HBF are land supply, housing targets, flexibility over planning and grants and loans for the sector, and they have been remarkably effective in delivering for their members in all these areas. They supported and helped to formulate Conservative government planning and housing policies in the 2010s, for example, the NPPF in 2012, the viability assessment of planning obligations (see Chapter 6) and the Help to Buy mortgage scheme – three of the most controversial areas of housing and planning policy. The HBF claim that they were responsible for the inclusion in the 2012 NPPF and in NPPF 2019 the contentious five-year supply of deliverable housing land referred to earlier (DCLG, 2012; MHCLG, 2019a).

The HBF has also been successful in persuading government examiners of local plans to resist local authority attempts to reduce government housing targets, and, in fact, have urged that, in many cases, the targets should be increased. Furthermore, since 2010, even during austerity for mainstream public services, they have been sensationally successful in getting billions of government funding directed into Help to Buy, development land reclamation and new infrastructure. They have also been able to persuade the government that local authorities should submit to developer pressure on housing affordability targets, planning standards and low-carbon design. The innovative 2007 Code Level for housing design aimed at making new homes more carbon efficient was effectively scrapped by the government in 2015 after pressure from the housebuilders, just months before the zero–carbon Code Level 6 was to go live.

On the issue of land value capture, the HBF does not accept that the government creates value in land by its investment in infrastructure or that the government has a right to capture some of the uplift later for the wider community. Although this point of view flies in the face of the evidence that, for example transport investments have pushed up land values around rail stations and interchanges, the HBF still contends that these windfalls do not require additional government action. Just like the CLA, they say that windfall profits are already captured by capital gains tax or planning gain measures such as CIL or Section 106 agreements; no other action is required.

It goes further than this. Despite the shortage of affordable housing and the manipulation of the planning system by the big developers, the HBF does not accept the government's characterisation of the housing market as 'broken' or that, perhaps, the housing market mechanism or the volume housebuilding business itself might just bear some responsibility for the inadequate supply of new housing. Rather, the HBF regards local authorities as the primary cause of low levels of housebuilding and of prohibitive prices for the many. They claim that the housing shortage is caused by local authorities not allocating enough land for housing and asking for too much from planning obligations and CIL charges.

The central contradiction in the HBF platform is that at the same time as wanting the state to reduce its control over development, they lobby for more state subsidies and government intervention to support their business model and profit margins. Some examples of this are:

- Putting pressure on local authorities in the local plan process to allocate more land for housing through the planning system.
- Pressing for the continuation of Help to Buy. The HBF are not the only parts of the property lobby that are saying this, for example, the Construction Products Association in 2018 issued a 'dire warning that house building will start to decline next year unless the Help to Buy is extended beyond 2021' (Champ, 2018).
- Lobbying for more government funding to improve construction skills. The HBF argue that the country does not have enough skilled workers to deliver the government target of 300,000 new homes per annum and wants the government to set up more construction training programmes.
- Lobbying for more flexibility on planning policy. The HBF believe that it has been successful in shaping the national planning guidance of the Coalition government of 2010 and Conservative governments

of 2015 and 2017; indeed, it wants the government to go further to loosen restrictions on development.

- Lobbying to retain viability testing in the planning system. The HBF believes that it was able to get the 2010 government to introduce the controversial viability testing policy into planning. It does not want this test to be removed and, indeed, it was retained in the amended versions of the NPPF in 2018 and 2019.
- Lobbying for the flexible treatment of planning obligations by local authorities. The HBF wants to make sure that Section 106 obligations for affordable housing or CIL charges are not increased. In other words, they should be formulated to meet developer requirements rather than meeting the needs of the public.

This lobby activity by the HBF protects very precisely the components of the housebuilders' business models. The central requirement of the model is to restrict the supply of housing in order to keep up prices, and to use the ensuing housing shortage to lobby for more land to be allocated for housing in order to incorporate it into their land banks. In response to the specific threats to land banking from the Callcutt review of housebuilding in 2007 and the Letwin review of build-out rates in 2018, the HBF and other lobby groups have been able to block suggestions about measures that would force landowners to put housing development land on the market or place restrictions on the drip-feeding of newbuild homes. The Callcutt Review concluded that 'there is no evidence of housebuilders holding onto land longer than they need ... and government should not take general measures to force rapid build out of land banks with implementable planning permissions' (Callcutt, 2007: 390). The Letwin study ten years later largely ignored the evidence of drip feeding and land banking and concluded that 'it would not be sensible to attempt to solve the problem of market absorption rates by forcing the major housebuilders to reduce their prices' (Letwin, 2018, para 1.8). Letwin concluded that there was no evidence that speculative land banking was part of the business model of the major house builders.

The second key requirement of the business model is to obtain as much subsidy as possible through government Help to Buy, and grants and loans for infrastructure in order to reduce their upfront costs. As we have seen, the government has been only too willing to offer this support because it wants to show that it is stimulating housebuilding and supporting homeownership.

The third requirement of the business model is to limit planning gain contributions, particularly requirements over the provision of affordable housing. Again, the sector has been highly successful in its approaches to the government, which opened the door to viability assessment in 2012 – with consequent significant reductions in affordable housing. There was a moment in 2017/18 when the government was faced with a barrage of criticism in the media and by housing charities such as Shelter and the Joseph Rowntree Foundation about the disastrous impact of viability assessments on affordable housing contributions, and there might have been an opportunity to drop it. The HBF and others urged the government to stand firm. Viability assessment was modified but survived in the revised NPPF 2018 and 2019 (MHCLG, 2018, 2019a).

Landlords

Privately rented property is the fastest-growing part of the housing market. The relentless rise in house prices and reduction in social and affordable housing has driven many more households into the private rented sector. This has been fuelled by Buy to Let, Right to Buy, caps on Housing Benefit payments and Build to Rent The private rented sector is now catering for all levels of income and is a significant investment sector for landlords and developers.

According to the grass-roots pressure group Generation Rent, private landlords make a staggering £77.7 billion each year in rent payments and capital gains. Of this, £9.3 billion comes straight from the government in Housing Benefit payments, with landlords also benefitting from £26.7 billion in tax breaks.[6]

The private rented sector has been extremely successful in fending off regulation, particularly the threat of rent controls, the expansion of tenant rights or the comprehensive quality control of rented properties. Yet, the landlord lobby has been able to successfully plead for generous tax breaks, ironically based on the claim that if the government ignores their demands, more people will be on the streets.

The largest landlord lobby is the Residential Landlord Association (RLA) which claims to have 30,000 members covering 250,000 properties. It has been in existence of 20 years. It has an active political campaigning arm, meeting ministers, undertaking research and issuing regular press releases about perceived threats to the private rented sector and Buy to Let landlords. For example, it ran a campaign against proposed tax measures to limit the booming Buy to Let market in the 2010s. In 2017, the RLA's website stated that:

> Last year saw an unprecedented attack on the Private Rented Sector, with former Chancellor George Osborne

announcing a raft of tax changes designed to hit buy-to-let landlords in the pocket. The tax raid shook the very foundations of the sector at a time when the Government is more reliant than ever on private landlords to provide the rental homes that are so desperately needed across the country. A 3 per cent stamp duty surcharge was introduced on the purchase of buy-to-let properties and Mortgage Interest Relief will be cut to basic rate tax progressively from 2017. Capital Gains Tax changes are in the pipeline too. It is clear that the PRS is being treated as a cash cow by the treasury. But the RLA is fighting back, lobbing at the very highest level to make changes.[7]

Recent RLA campaigns focus on opposing legislation that would give more rights to tenants. Thus, its response to proposals to give tenants three-year tenancies, which were widely supported by front-line housing groups like Shelter and Crisis, was a fierce rejection:

> We would warn against making it a statutory requirement to introduce three year tenancies. Many tenants simply do not want to be tied to a property long term. It is vital that the market is able to provide the flexibility that many need in order to swiftly access new work and educational opportunities. (RLA, 2018)

However, the RLA added, rather cynically, that it might accept three-year tenancies if landlords were offered tax relief incentives. Similarly, when proposals were floated to allow tenants the right to buy privately rented properties, the landlords argued for tax relief for that as well. Thus, landlords will give way on proposals they do not like if they are paid large sums by the Treasury – never mind that over the past eight years, private rents have rocketed and landlords' profits have risen spectacularly.

Proposals by the Mayor of London to introduce rent controls in the capital after the mayoral election of 2020 have caused outrage in the RLA and in government circles. As ever, they claim that controls would reduce the size of the rental market – never mind that the mayor's proposals actually allow rents to rise in a controlled way, and that the profits of landlords are extraordinary in London due to exceptionally high rents. The Centre for Policy Studies weighed in with the following defence of landlords: 'Landlords aren't a class of social parasites they are mostly elderly people who are seeking basic returns to live off in their old age' (Colville, 2019). When some of the biggest residential landlords in London are the largest landowners and property companies in the UK, who are they kidding?

While the organised landlord lobby is a potent force, it is not on its own. We must not forget that landlords also have support where it matters – in the House of Commons. Research has shown that one in five, or 123, MPs rent out property and, for this reason, have a vested interest in legislation that affects lands and tenants.[8] You can imagine their response to rent controls in London, where most of their rental units are located.

Commercial property

Two of the most vocal bodies for commercial real estate are the BPF and the Association of Real Estate Funds (AREF), recently merged with the Investment Association. BPF members are primarily developers and professional bodies engaged in development, while AREF members are one stage removed fund managers who are not involved in development. Both groups carry significant weight with the government.

The British Property Federation (BPF)

The BPF is the principal lobby for commercial real estate. Historically, it has had an indirect relationship with housing development and national housing policy, but this is changing as commercial investors look more closely at residential for investment opportunities via Build to Rent and large mixed-use urban regeneration schemes. Although the BPF does not represent the volume housebuilders, it works closely with the HBF and the CLA on a range of planning and land policy and taxation issues. BPF lobby activity targets national government policy, aiming to influence high-level policy. However, it does not operate at the local or regional levels, as do the CLA and the HBF, who engage directly in local planning and housing.

The BPF was formed in 1963. It has 400 members, of which: 31 per cent are commercial real estate companies, including some the largest in the UK; 9 per cent are institutional investors; 36 per cent are professional firms such as lawyers and the major surveying companies, 3 per cent are investment banks; and 3 per cent are public utilities and semi-public landowners such as the Crown Estate. The BPF has recently attracted membership from foreign investors and wealth funds. Their members include the major REITs, as well as the largest pension funds such as Hermes (the former Post Office superannuation fund) and the big property consultants such as the CBRE, BNP Paribas and Savills. Hence, they are a powerful lobby with membership across the commercial property investment, development and professional sector.

BPF lobby methods include meeting ministers, making submissions to government consultations, attending political party conferences and issuing regular press releases. Establishing personal relationships with key politicians is critical. The BPF does not publish a house magazine, but they commission research and surveys that are used for lobbying and the promotion of their point of view.

Their key housing lobby issues are:

- Build to Rent. The most important current housing policy issue for the BPF, Build to Rent has been promoted by them for some years and is now accelerating. The BPF claims success in influencing the review of barriers to institutional investment in private rented homes in 2012 undertaken by Sir Adrian Montague. This led to the appointment of a dedicated private rented sector champion, Mark Davis, inside the Department of Communities and Local Government (DCLG) to deliver the recommendations of the Montague review. BPF research in 2018 found that 75 per cent of MPs believe that the Build to Rent sector will help to increase housing supply.[9]
- Planning guidance. The BPF is positive about national planning policy overall. It claims specific success in getting two pages of guidance on Build to Rent in the 2018 update of the NPPF. Given the small contribution of Build to Rent to housing supply, this is quite some achievement. For the same reason, the BPF supports the recently announced 'housing delivery test' aimed at local authorities meeting housing targets, in which the BPF hope that Build to Rent will be a growing category.
- Stamp Duty Land Tax (SDLT). SDLT is paid on property or land purchases over £125,000 and over £150,000 for non-residential purchases. In 2011, the government proposed an SDLT surcharge of 3 per cent for those buying more than one property. This is not an unreasonable measure, but it led to protests from the BPF, who sought an opt-out for institutional investors (even though, as we have seen, many property companies operate through trusts that are exempt from the surcharge). In the event, the BPF failed to get the opt-out.
- Land value capture. Like the CLA, LPDF and HBF, the BPF strongly opposes additional measures of land taxation or the introduction of 'use it or lose it' measures. For example, on 13

September 2018, the BPF issued a press release with the headline; 'Land Value Capture reform will stifle much needed investment in communities and will stunt housing delivery'.[10] Existing levels of Section 106 and CIL charges are acceptable but nothing more. The familiar threat, echoing the CLA, is that if more value is captured for the community, landowners will hold land off the market and institutions will not invest.

- The BPF supports the viability testing of local plans. It thinks the right approach is that of the Mayor of London, who requires a viability test only if developers refuse to offer the percentage of affordable housing (35 per cent) set down in the mayor's housing policy.

The Association of Real Estate Funds

The AREF is quite different from the BPF. It is an association of property fund managers that aims to lobby policymakers on behalf of the real estate fund industry (mainly commercial property). It claims a membership of 65 members, with a total of £72 billion under management. Its committees cover all aspects of finance and taxation concerned with property investment. For example, it lobbied the government to resist the 3 per cent SDLT levy on property transactions, claiming that it would add 4 per cent to the costs of transferring property portfolios among investors.

In 2019, the AREF announced that they were joining forces with the even larger Investment Association (which also describes itself as a trade body), which has a mere £7.7 trillion in assets, in order to provide backup if there are fund withdrawals due to Brexit shocks in the future.

UK Finance

Many banks, financial institutions, building societies and investment funds are big enough to lobby ministers or officials directly face to face, or to employ lobby specialists to do it for them. It also works the other way, with governments courting the banking and finance sector directly, on a regular basis, to gain support for their policies. In addition, many banks and finance companies also belong to trade groups that seek to coordinate the response of the UK finance sector. These include UK Finance, the British Private Equity and Venture Capital Association (BVCA) and the Association of Foreign Banks. The Association of Mortgage Lenders was integrated into UK Finance in

2017. In this chapter, we focus on UK Finance as the most prominent of these lobby groups.

UK Finance (known as the British Bankers Association until 2017) describes itself as a trade association with 300 companies in banking, finance and credit. UK Finance issues daily news releases and commentaries, including numerous releases on mortgage finance. It is in the area of mortgage finance and overall levels of property investment that the banking lobby is most instrumental in shaping government land and housing policy.

The key property lobby issues of UK Finance are:

- Mortgage finance. Given the critical importance of mortgages to the UK economy (£23.5 billion of gross mortgage debt in 2018), mortgage debt and interest rates are a principal concern of the banking lobby, as are housing policies that are related to them. The merger of the Association of Mortgage Lenders with UK Finance in 2017 is a further demonstration of the critical importance of mortgage finance to the whole financial system. After reckless 'sub-prime' mortgage lending brought the banking sector down in 2008, the banks (and the government) are now taking mortgage debt much more seriously. Close monitoring of mortgage debt and better 'due diligence', as well as new bank capitalisation requirements, have reduced the risk of another collapse, but as one banking insider told the author, the banks have "a herd instinct", so the danger is still there.
- The stability of the commercial and housebuilding property market. Given that land and property make up 80 per cent of the asset base of the banks, acting as collateral for almost every loan, the finance system is heavily reliant on growth in land and property prices over the long and short term. As my insider told me "The banks always believe the market is going up." There is a big risk to the banks and the economy if they misjudge this and land and property prices fall.
- Taxation of property is a major preoccupation. UK Finance has lobbied the government over retaining Help to Buy and reducing SDLT because they are perceived to affect the health of the housing market and property investment market.
- QE was strongly supported by the banks in the 2000s. It allowed them to increase their loan capacity after the financial crash but a substantial number of these loans were to property development and investment, so their dependency on the property market has continued.
- Funding residential development. This is hugely important to the banks. They make loans to both the private housebuilding sector

and housing associations. They made £8.6 billion available for social housing in 2017 (mainly to housing associations). UK Finance thus welcomed government announcements in 2018 that it would be putting more government money into the affordable housing sector since this would be matched with funding from the banks and other finance institutions. It added: 'UK Finance and its members now stand ready to work with the government and housing associations to support long-term investment in affordable homes'.[11]

The property lobby in local government

Local councils are the front line of planning and development. This is where the day-to-day decisions about development take place. It is both highly technical and political. Local councillors are required to grant (or refuse) consent on countless planning applications every week, and to approve local plans and statutory policies on housing, land and landlord regulation.

In response to accusations that councillors were making planning decisions on 'political grounds', the Nolan report (1997) on *Standards of conduct in local government* in 1997 and subsequent guidance from the Local Government Association in 2013 accepted that, while it was difficult to separate out political criteria from planning criteria, they recommended that councillors who are on planning committees should only make decisions on 'valid planning grounds' (LGA, 2013). However, since much of town planning is inherently political, it is almost impossible to define precisely a valid planning ground or how this is different from a political consideration.

The politicisation of planning, which is inevitable, must not be confused with corruption. Although according to Nolan the UK planning system is not financially corrupt, there is an ever-present danger of undue influence by special interests. This is more commonplace as there is continuous lobbying of council officers and members by applicants for planning permission. Although protocols on the direct lobbying of councillors and officers have been tightened up in recent years after Nolan reported, chairs of planning committees routinely meet up with developers to discuss planning applications. Ideally, these meetings should only take place with officers of the council present, though some senior politicians ignore this. There are no data on the impact of these contacts on decisions, but it would be surprising if they had no impact. Occasional articles in local newspapers and *Private Eye* reveal extreme examples of familiarity between councillors and developers.

The case of Mr Robert Davis hit the headlines in 2017. He was chairman of Westminster City Council Planning Committee for six years, over which period he received hospitality or gifts 893 times. These included trips to the South of France and to expensive dinners paid for by developers who were seeking planning permission from Westminster Council. These gifts were not declared as they should have been according to the council's own code of conduct, and he should have stood aside from key decisions on the grounds that he may have had a conflict of interest. In 2018, he resigned after an internal investigation found that he had breached the council's code of conduct. The investigation found no evidence that the hospitality he received influenced planning decisions by the council, but it nevertheless gave the impression of corrupt relationships (Booth, 2018). This case demonstrates that even 20 years after the Nolan report, there are cases of misconduct taking place in plain sight that continue because they are protected by party loyalties.

Another case involving Westminster City Council uncovered by the *Daily Mirror* (Sommerlad, 2019) amounted to a corrupt relationship between politicians and developers. In 2016, the council gave planning permission for a £100 million development of Millbank Tower, comprising luxury housing and a boutique hotel. Despite planning officers suggesting that the developer should make a £57 million financial contribution for affordable housing, the council decided on no contribution and zero affordable housing. The Mayor of London at the time was Boris Johnson, who agreed to the zero contribution. Later, Boris Johnson accepted £50,000 in donations from the developer. The developer is listed as the second-richest person in the UK in the *Sunday Times* rich list.

Of equal importance is the well-documented revolving door between local authorities, consultants and developers. Council officers have moved seamlessly from council service into consultancies that are working for clients on development projects in their local authority area. Councillors have second jobs working as advisers and lobbyists for property companies working in their own or adjoining council areas. This has an insidious impact, making it easier for developers armed with this inside knowledge to receive planning consents through the local authority system, giving the impression that some councillors are not representing their constituents, but acting as promoters for developers.

Anna Minton published a report in 2017 at the height of major planning disputes in the borough of Southwark over the lack of affordable housing from new development. This report showed that an astonishing 20 per cent of Southwark Council's 63 councillors in the Labour-controlled borough were employed as lobbyists related to the development sector.[12] Nor was this an exceptional case. A *Guardian* investigation found that almost one in ten councillors in London either work for property businesses or have received gifts or hospitality from them: 'Nearly 100 councillors in the capital work for property companies or lobbying and communications consultancies involved in planning, according to declarations of interest made by elected representatives. Some of them also sit on planning committees making decisions over major developments, including volumes of affordable housing' (Booth and Crossley, 2018).

Political party donations and interests

The Conservative Party is historically assumed, rightly, to be the party of land and property, and this relationship continues to the present day. In 2011, the *Daily Telegraph* (Blake, 2011) reported that over the previous three years, the Conservative Party had been given £3.3 million by property developers 'that stand to benefit from Conservative planning reforms'. Bisnow website reported that this access is assisted by the Conservative Party Property Forum which enables developers and landowners to pay £2,500 per annum for access to dinners and drinks with Ministers (Phillips, 2017). The same report listed ten property developers who bankrolled the 2017 election to the tune of £1 million. One example is Bruce Ritchie, owner of the Residential Land Group, which owns 1,200 privately rented properties in Central London plus hotels. According to Wikipedia, he and his wife have given £750,000 to the Conservative Party, including donations to a campaign against the imposition of a proposed mansion tax. He is co-chair of the notorious Presidents Club for wealthy Tory donors and has personally paid £50,000 to dine with the prime minister.

Several prominent MPs engaged in policy decisions on land and taxation at the highest level are themselves property developers, commercial landlords or major landowners. For example, Philip Hammond, Chancellor of the Exchequer in the May government, owns a property company and has an option agreement with a housebuilder for green belt land close to his home in Surrey that can benefit from a relaxation of the controls over green belt development (Myers, 2017). Jeremy Hunt, Foreign Secretary in the May government, is also an active property speculator. In 2017, he 'bulk purchased' seven luxury flats from a Conservative donor in Southampton Ocean Village to cash in on the Buy to Let business and avoided £100,000 of stamp duty surcharge because he bought more than six properties which under rules created by his own government are exempt from the surcharge (Gregory, 2018).

Other MPs are major landowners and exert their influence on policy through their ownerships and connections. Shrubsole (2019: 19) cites the case of Richard Benyon, former MP for Newbury, who was the richest MP in Parliament. Benyon owns a 12,000-acre estate in Berkshire that is classified as a family-controlled charitable trust, thus avoiding taxes. He also owns an 8,000-acre grouse moor in Scotland. His estates attract significant farming subsidies. Despite, or perhaps because of these interests, Benyon was made Wildlife Minister by David Cameron. His parliamentary activities have been described by George Monbiot in *The Guardian* (Monbiot, 2012) as 'repeatedly wielding his power in ways that promote his own interests'. Shrubsole refers to other landed MPs such as Richard Drax, Henry Bellingham and Richard Clifton-Brown, who own large country estates and are also happy to pocket large farming subsidies. Many other MPs act as consultants to property companies or receive donations from property companies. So extensive are Conservative links to property that there is a Conservative National Property Advisory Committee affiliated to the Conservative Party offering professional help to party members on their own property issues.

Conclusion

A picture has been painted of a property lobby of immense power and influence that has effectively got the government and, most particularly, the Conservative Party where it wants them. Although the property world is made up of many different actors, landowners, investors and volume housebuilders, these interests share a common aim to protect the market in land and property. They all broadly agree on the following agenda: less land and property taxation; rising prices; less planning gain; more planning deregulation; and more government intervention to help out the market.

However, there are differences of focus. The free-market CLA is more overtly political than the RICS. The BPF represents investors and commercial property developers mainly in London and the South East, and has less interest in the housing crisis. The LPDF is closely focused on fighting off taxation and land value capture on sites that are being promoted for residential development. The HBF is concerned with newbuild market housing, not landlord regulation.

Some parts of the industry, for example, landlords and the volume housebuilders, have an overall poor public image and, despite their influence, are on the defensive. Even the BPF complains that the government does not appreciate what commercial development does to help the economy. Landlords feel beleaguered by government regulation. UK Finance is also trying to repair its image after the 2008 financial crash in which the banks were widely blamed for bringing down the economy through reckless lending for property.

In spite of its success in protecting the property market and seeing off state intervention in land and taxation, the property lobby does not always get its way. It depends on the receptiveness of the government at the national and local levels, and on the strength of public opinion. The property sector overall is openly partisan about supporting Conservative governments and the Conservative Party. It fears that left-wing governments will push back against the property lobby and disrupt the market. However, at the micro-level of local planning decisions, success for the property lobby is not guaranteed. Market forces will normally get their way on development proposals, even where there is strong local opposition, but not always. Huge profits are at stake over planning decisions and this is why the property sector is prepared to commit so many resources into lobbying and advocacy at the national level to ensure that the national planning and taxation framework works for them. Most governments take notice when the large development companies or finance groups come knocking at the door. Moreover, lobbying is often the other way around, with government at both the central and local levels actively asking landowners, developers and finance groups to come in and invest – and offering them incentives to do so.

Thus, the property lobby matters in the housing crisis because it keeps the views and interests of the land and property market in the minds of ministers and officials. The property industry makes it clear that it is indispensable and that the whole pack of cards of investment, growth and homeownership will fall apart without it – never mind that the property market caused the financial crash of 2008 and every boom and bust before that. The veiled threat of another collapse if support is withdrawn is also aimed at stopping any interventions that would undermine their dominance and profit margins. Yet, this power over politicians is, of course, precisely the danger that the property lobby poses to the UK and to the housing chances of many millions facing housing stress.

There is an argument that the financial crash has damaged the reputation of the banks and finance houses – the 'masters of the universe' – in the City of London and that the corporate business lobby therefore has less purchase with government and the public.

There may have been some truth to this in the immediate aftermath of the financial crash. Now, this is largely forgotten. In the examples of the property lobby in action over housing policy before and after the financial crash, which we explore in Chapter 6, the property lobby remains as powerful as ever.

6

Shaping national housing and planning policy

So far, this book has explored finance, housing and planning from the perspective of overall national housing policy. This chapter turns to three detailed examples of how the finance–housebuilding complex has decisively influenced specific national policies on housing and planning. The rise and rise of the property lobby is not always in plain sight at the level of national policymaking, or at the local level, because its influence is obscured by legal and technical jargon and by high-level political lobbying.

The following examples demonstrate how important it is to open up the assumptions and practices of the property sector and its relationship to the government at the national and local levels to public examination. Inside each example lies a truth about the impasse that we have reached about housing, and about the need to do things very differently if the nation is to have any chance of meeting the needs of all those who have a right to housing.

New Labour's Growth Areas programme, 2000–10

In this first case study, we are going back to the period before the financial crash of 2008. This retrospective is relevant because it helps to explain why the housing crisis is not simply a consequence of having Conservative governments or a financial crash – though they have made things very much worse. The housing crisis is more systemic than that and understanding how the finance/property system works across governments of all colours helps to explain why we are so stuck when it comes to tackling it.

The period of New Labour governments between 1997 and 2010 casts a light on how the Labour Party approached the problem of planning for housing growth. In 1997, New Labour had significant economic and political flexibility when it came into office. The economy was picking up and was soon to enter a boom period, Labour had a large parliamentary majority and it had spent years in opposition in the 1990s working up detailed plans to tackle the housing crisis. It was prepared to spend government money (with some important limitations, as discussed later) and allow local government to take the lead in regeneration and rebuilding public services. It also had ambitious plans for regional government and strategic infrastructure. Labour had a socially and environmentally interventionist housing and planning tradition, which included a spatial-planning and a market-directing approach. There was also enthusiasm in Whitehall and across the country for mainstreaming sustainability and sustainable development throughout the government. Tackling climate change was a positive idea with citizens' movements active locally and nationally. A new dawn seemed possible.

In the housing sector, it was recognised by the government and communities that there was huge unmet demand for both market and affordable housing, and there was much to be done to upgrade the existing housing stock. There was willingness, indeed, excitement in local authorities, developers and housing associations to work with communities and the government to get housebuilding moving. The government was committed to a comprehensive approach: building more affordable housing; repairing run-down council estates and deprived neighbourhoods; and housing the homeless. At this time, town planning was not demonised; on the contrary, it was seen by the government as an essential mechanism to deliver more housing and sustainable development. National and regional planning was viewed as a positive mechanism to ensure that all areas of the country benefitted from new housing growth and from government funding for the renewal of the public housing stock.

The ambition was set out by Deputy Prime Minister John Prescott in the Sustainable Communities Plan (SCP) in 2003. The SCP called for housing action on all fronts, including a major programme of estate renewal across the country, and new housebuilding in four Growth Areas: Milton Keynes; South Midlands; the Thames Gateway; the London–Stansted–Cambridge corridor; and Ashford in Kent. The Growth Areas were estimated to have potential for 200,000 extra homes above existing targets. Moreover, the SCP aimed to build 'new communities rather than housing estates', and even more than that, to make sure they were 'sustainable communities'. Each new community would be environmentally, socially and economically sustainable in terms of employment, transport, green construction methods and public services. A sum of £600 million was allocated to the Growth Areas for infrastructure for 2001–05. Local delivery vehicles or partnership boards were set up for each of the Growth Areas – the government would work together with local authorities and developers to deliver new housing (Cochrane et al, 2015).

When the Growth Areas were announced, villages and small towns in the Growth Areas, particularly those with Conservative councils, accused John Prescott of wanting to 'build over the countryside'. However, the SCP commitment to sustainable development was expected to overcome this resistance because it aimed to ensure that public services, green space and quality design would accompany new housing development. It would not be housing estates first and public services later as an afterthought, as was the norm up to this point. The day of faceless new housing estates was over.

However, there was one fatal flaw with the New Labour plan: the delivery of sustainable communities relied overwhelmingly on existing landowners and the volume housebuilders, with physical and social infrastructure being funded from the profits of housing development and from government investment. Landowners would release land and private developers would build most of the new homes. It was the opposite strategy to the new towns of an earlier period of planned growth in the South East, when central government bought the land and built on it with its own resources through new town development corporations. The SCP was founded on a very different model: public–private partnerships, with the state providing a framework and funds for infrastructure, and the market delivering new housing. Although some land in the Growth Areas was in the hands of English Partnerships, no additional land would need to be purchased by compulsory purchase and little would need to be spent on public housing or community facilities because the market would do the job of delivering a range of housing types and tenures and deliver community facilities as planning gain from their developments.

Oddly, in the SCP documents, the words 'landowners' or 'volume housebuilders' were not used. Instead, the SCP talked of 'partners and stakeholders', a phraseology that rather underestimated and hid the unequal relationship that actually existed in the delivery partnerships. The private partners had no difficulty agreeing to the Growth Area plans; indeed, they were delighted because the plans allocated large areas of land for new housing in the South East of England, easily the most profitable housing market area in the country. Research into the Growth Areas revealed that at the numerous Growth Area board meetings in Whitehall with the partners, the government offered funding for infrastructure (mainly new roads) to open up housing development sites, with few questions asked about what the housebuilders would deliver in return (Open University, 2017).

The government was impatient to meet housing targets and get housing built as fast as possible; consequently, civil servants, ministers and local government officials in attendance at these meetings failed to pin down the conditions of engagement. For example, what would be the price of the land and the homes? Which sites would be built out first? What would be the build-out rates? How much affordable housing would be provided as planning gain? Who would pay for community facilities? What would happen to housing targets and affordable housing if the market slowed down? There was no clear idea of the consequences for the housebuilders if, after receipt of government pump-priming funds and planning consents, they did not meet government housing targets. Whitehall gave them a blank cheque – without interrogating their business model. The government had no plan B if the builders did not deliver, or if the housing market crashed. Worse still, communities who were promised sustainable communities were not invited to these crucial Whitehall meetings, nor were proceedings made public, yet these meetings determined the fate of the Growth Areas.

In the event, the financial crash stopped the Growth Areas programme in its tracks in 2008/09. However, it had five years to run before that, and already by 2007/08, it was obvious that the government's Growth Area housing targets were far too optimistic. New housing starts were below target and building sustainable communities proved to be much more complex and costly than thought. As for the housebuilders, they saw no value premium from building low-carbon homes and relatively little from the other sustainable development measures that the government was asking for. The builders noted that house prices did not go up if a new community was designed as a 'sustainable community'. The extra costs and special features, such as sustainable drainage systems (SUDS) or low-carbon technologies, did not produce extra profit or a premium on house prices. In fact, there was very limited market demand for low-carbon homes (measured as Code Level 6 on the government scale of low-carbon technology) and there were extra burdens for homeowners in managing these technologies that made the homes more difficult to sell. Thus, house prices in sustainable communities were immune to sustainability innovations. In any case, the housebuilders did not see delivering sustainable development as their responsibility. Since it brought no market advantage, they carried on building to their conventional business model.

Moreover, all was not well in Whitehall with its side of the bargain. Essential strategic infrastructure, such as widening motorways or building major roads to enable sites to be developed, was delayed or not funded. A case in point was the years of delay in widening the strategic A14 in Northamptonshire to open up large development sites alongside it. The Department of Transport was not fully committed to the transport schemes listed in the SCP, and as for new doctors' surgeries and hospitals, they depended upon NHS funding that was not within the power of ministers responsible for housing and planning. Despite the fanfare of the SCP and lobbying of Whitehall by local authorities, there were no promises of additional revenue funding for public services as populations grew in the Growth Areas. It turned out that the Growth Areas had not been fully factored into the Treasury revenue expenditure plans or into the capital programmes of government departments that were essential to making sustainable communities a reality. The costings in the SCP were just that – costings on paper, not firm commitments. The term current at the time used to describe this bureaucratic tangle was that 'the government was not joined up'. Unfortunately it was true.

The SCP has been described as a strategy of 'utopian optimism' (Cochrane et al, 2015). The government believed that it could get a win–win: the builders would deliver thousands of new homes; and would also deliver from their profits the affordable housing and sustainable communities that the government and local authorities wanted. In other words, the government would pump-prime by making land and strategic infrastructure available, and the housebuilders would do the rest. It was a parallel with New Labour's Faustian pact with the City of London: by fattening the golden goose, the goose would be content to deliver for society.

In reality, this was denial on a huge scale. Enough had been written and researched over the previous 20 years to demonstrate that the finance–housebuilding complex was powerful and strongly profit focused. It was expert at 'playing' the government to get what it wanted (Ball, 1983; Short et al, 1986). The property lobby was already well organised by the time of the SCP. In fact, the formulation of the SCP and the Growth Areas win–win formula was one of the biggest successes of the property lobby in their campaign for more land to be released for housing. However, in denying the reality of the housebuilders' and landowners' business model, with its tight focus on profit margins and shareholder value, the New Labour Growth Area vision of a win–win partnership was a fantasy. Labour 'overpromised' and paid the price when many of the parliamentary seats in the Growth Areas went Conservative in 2010.

The Labour government should have learned the lessons of the new towns and stepped in with a programme of land acquisition of the key housing sites in the Growth Areas in order to enable them to take control of the development process and ensure that sustainable communities were delivered. Where they did own sites through English Partnerships, government agencies or local authorities should have built on them directly rather than parcelling out land to the volume housebuilders to build them out to their own timescale. Interviews by the author during research on the Growth Areas revealed that at meetings in London between officials of the Growth Area strategic partnerships and government ministers responsible for the Growth Areas, the government was made aware of the weakness of the Growth Areas approach as it emerged in the mid-2000s. In fact, ministers were frustrated at progress and demanded that targets be met, blaming the local authorities and strategic partnerships to being too slow. In coded language, these exhortations meant 'forget sustainable communities, just get homes built'. The West Northants Development Corporation (WNDC), for example, was responsible for delivering a number of housing sites around Daventry and Northampton, many in private ownership. The WNDC was entirely dependent on the landowners and volume housebuilders for the delivery of large numbers of new homes and for their quality. Insiders in the WNDC told researchers that the housebuilders were "impossible to deal with", producing poorly designed standard housing estate schemes devoid of the content and imagination of sustainable communities, but the WNDC had no powers or money to force them to change their model – and the government would not give the WNDC any more funding or powers (Cochrane et al, 2015).

The lesson from the New Labour Growth Areas is that the government cannot leave the resolution of the housing crisis to the volume housebuilders or the landowners nor to a weakened planning system. The government and communities must own and control housing development land in order to deliver what people need and want at a local level. The developers and landowners were able to run rings round New Labour at both the national and local levels. The hard lesson is that the finance–housebuilding complex is driven by short-term profit margins. They are single-purpose housebuilding organisations, not sustainable community or town planning organisations. The government cannot expect them to deliver sustainable development or affordable housing. Their shareholders do not invest in them to solve the housing crisis or plan sustainable communities. Unfortunately, New Labour did not have the political will or inside knowledge to deal with them effectively – and had no plan B up its sleeve.

As a footnote, it should be mentioned that the SCP and the Growth Areas were wound up when the Coalition government entered power in 2010. It wound them up not because they did not deliver, but because they were seen by the Coalition as an ideological exercise in undemocratic central government power over local communities. The irony of this is that contrary to Coalition government statements, many local authorities and communities in the Growth Areas actually supported the strategic partnerships because they wanted housing growth to revitalise public services, housing stock and town centres in their districts.

Somewhat cynically, the HBF changed its tune from supporting the Growth Areas in the 2000s because it benefited its members, to saying that they had no objection to winding up the Growth Areas in 2010. They sided with the Coalition line that the Growth Areas were too bureaucratic and restrictive when, in fact, it was precisely this bureaucracy that had delivered land and multiple planning consents for their members. The problem with delivery was that the housebuilders did not fulfil their side of the bargain. In Northamptonshire, many of the sites granted planning permission under the SCP were, in fact, never started or fully built out by the housebuilders five years later (Cochrane et al, 2015).

The National Planning Policy Framework (NPPF) 2012 and its capture by the property lobby

The second example of the influence of the finance–housebuilding complex over government planning and housing policy is the drafting of the NPPF published in 2012 by the Coalition government (DCLG, 2012). This section of the book draws on the work of Andrew Slade (2018), who wrote his PhD on the evolution of the NPPF from the point of view of how government formulates policy.

The Conservatives in opposition in the 2000s had long wanted a more decentralised and market-led town planning system (Conservative Party, 2010). Notwithstanding that New Labour, as we have seen in the previous example, was dependent on the housebuilders to deliver new housing, the Conservative Party perception was that the planning system was top-down and directed by Whitehall. Its new pitch to voters was smaller government activated by localism and the Big Society. This was a potentially popular position directed at voters in the shire counties, but how did this stand with the developers?

After the financial crash and in a climate of cutbacks in public spending, the Coalition (in particular, the Treasury) demanded that town planning should be reoriented from a regulatory system to the out-and-out promotion of economic growth (HM Treasury, 2011). However, this imperative of letting the housebuilders build when and where they wanted had to be reconciled with the new localism agenda, and for that to happen, limits had to be placed on the power of localism to stop development.

The drafting of the NPPF from 2010 to its publication in 2012 demonstrates how the Coalition tried to square this circle. In particular, it shows how the housebuilders, backed by the Treasury, were able to ensure that their interests were given primacy. It started amazingly easily for them. The Conservatives created a Planning Sounding Board (PSB) in 2010 on the back of a number of think-tank reports on deregulating planning and decentralisation. The PSB included representatives of the development industry, Conservative councillors and a sprinkling of representatives of environmental groups, notably, the Royal Society for the Protection of Birds (the RSPB), which had support in Conservative circles. The PSB was chaired by John Howell MP, who had worked for Savills and was author of an influential Conservative Party (2010) report called *Open source planning*. The PSB was seen by Howell 'as largely self-selecting – there were a number of key players in the market and we just picked them all up' (Slade, 2018: 117). Their view was that the planning system was 'negative and adversarial' and local councils were regarded as 'part of the problem'. Nevertheless, there were tensions. Some influential Conservatives, notably, Oliver Letwin (later to author a report on the housebuilders in 2018), wanted to get rid of the local authority-determined plan-led system altogether and devolve planning straight down to communities. Others, including future Planning Minister Greg Clarke, were more pragmatic and were concerned that if there was too much upheaval in the planning system, the housebuilders might delay getting on with building (Slade, 2018: 137).

In any event, following the election of the Coalition government in 2010, a Practitioners Advisory Group (PAG) was set up to do a first draft of new national planning guidance. The PAG was established secretly and without normal recruitment processes for appointment to public sector posts. The civil service was not asked to participate. There were just four members of the PAG, all of whom had been on the PSB and had been in contact with the Conservative Party during its years in opposition. They were:

- Peter Andrew, director of land and property at Taylor Wimpey and, subsequently, in 2015, deputy chairman of the HBF. He is noted for 'going on about viability' (Slade, 2018: 156). He was given an MBE in 2018.
- John Rhodes, founder of QUOD consultants, a very pro-development consultancy. He received an MBE from David Cameron in 2015.

- Gary Porter, Conservative leader of South Holland Council in Lincolnshire, who became chair of the Local Government Association in 2015. He was given a life peerage by David Cameron in 2015, becoming Baron Porter of Spalding. He was famed for saying: 'I hate planners.'
- Simon Marsh, head of sustainable development at the RSPB, who was in the PAG to represent environmental interests. He was given an MBE by David Cameron in 2013.

Significantly, the organisations that represented the town planning profession, RTPI, the Planning Officers Society and the TCPA were not included, nor were the CPRE or other voluntary associations. They were seen as 'anti-developer' or 'pro- planning'. The PAG by contrast had a pro-development agenda (notwithstanding Simon Marsh's involvement) and was in regular contact with the HBF. Andrew Whittaker, planning director of the HBF, was the main channel of communication with the PAG. In an interview with Daniel Slade, Whittaker said that 'the PAG was signed up to what we wanted to deliver', and that Rhodes and Andrew were 'our reps' on the PAG (Slade, 2018: 149). John Rhodes of QUOD consultants, as the main drafter of the PAG version of the NPPF, was a particularly important ally of the housebuilders.

This developer bias was justified by ministers as ensuring buy-in to future planning policy by the development sector. According to Slade's study, the Treasury under Chancellor George Osborne took the view that 'planning controls thwarted competitiveness and growth' and pushed 'the most brash and deregulated position' and wanted 'the most red blooded version of the NPPF' (Slade, 2018: 179).

In the event, a draft NPPF was published by the government in 2011 based very closely on the PAG report. There was fierce opposition to the NPPF from environmental groups when the NPPF went out for consultation, mainly around the statement that 'the default answer to development should be yes'. Yet, following the formal consultation, the only significant change was the replacement of this provocative statement with the ambiguous 'presumption in favour of sustainable development'. The RTPI withdrew its opposition and praised the NPPF for retaining the plan-led planning system but missed the crucial paragraph 173 on viability assessment that the PAG and the housebuilders had been lobbying for. This was, as Slade (2018: 167) says a 'battle for the soul of the planning system', but one in which the decisive winners were the housebuilders.

The property lobby and viability assessment

The introduction of viability assessment into planning is one of the most significant shifts in planning policy and practice in the 60 years since the foundational Town and Country Planning Act 1947. The purpose of the UK town planning system was to create legally binding local plans that would allocate land for its 'best use' in the public interest. Planning applications would need to conform to local plans but no compensation would be given for those whose land could not be developed as they wished. In other words, the policies in approved plans, consulted on locally, would be the primary test of development proposals.

When the first comprehensive Planning Act came into being in 1947, the best use of land was defined in public interest terms. It was specifically *not* based on the best use of land from a profit or financial value point of view. Indeed, the profitability of land and development was not a legitimate 'planning reason' or 'material consideration' for granting or refusing planning permission, or for formulating the pattern of preferred land uses in local plans. Town and country planning was about society and the built environment, not personal or commercial gain.

That is broadly the way the system worked until the financial crash, and the election of the Coalition government of 2010. Although the development sector never favoured the system of 'planning gain' or 'planning obligations', it accepted it as a reality for over 50 years – until the 2008 financial crash. At that point, the property lobby brought pressure to bear on the Conservatives, then in opposition, to bring in the concept of viability assessment. The lobby argued that rules should be changed so that irrespective of what was said in approved local plans, planning obligations could be lowered if a developer could successfully demonstrate that planning obligations made his scheme unviable. This argument was given additional force and credibility by the 2008 financial crash and recession that followed it. Under these circumstances the Treasury view was that anything 'holding back development' should be removed.

In this atmosphere, the Conservatives and the Liberal Democrats, their Coalition partners, introduced into the 2012 NPPF the policy of the viability assessment of planning decisions. The short paragraph 173 formulated by the PAG in collaboration with the RICS and the HBF has caused untold damage to the integrity of the English planning system. Most critically, it has significantly reduced the amount of affordable housing delivered while, at the same time, bolstering housebuilder and landowner profits to record levels. The precise wording of the new policy reveals the radicalism of this measure:

> Pursuing sustainable development requires careful attention to viability and costs in plan-making and decision-taking. Plans should be deliverable. Therefore, the sites and the scale of development identified in the plan should not be subject to such a scale of obligations and policy burdens that their ability to be developed viably is threatened. To ensure viability, the costs of any requirements likely to be applied to development, such as requirements for affordable housing, standards, infrastructure contributions or other requirements should, when taking account of the normal cost of development and mitigation, provide competitive returns to a willing land owner and willing developer to enable the development to be deliverable. (NPPF (Ministry of Housing and Local Government), 2012: para 173)

The viability clause is an extraordinary reversal of the purpose of town planning. First, the 'viability' of a planning scheme was defined solely in financial terms: social and environmental viability were ignored. The test of the best use of land thus became financial – all other aspects of planning took second place. Finance trumps all other planning considerations. Second, the viability clause equates 'sustainable development' with the commercial viability of a development scheme. In effect, the financial viability of a scheme defines whether it can be considered sustainable development. Third, the third sentence in paragraph 173 says bluntly that local authorities should not place 'any obligations or policy burdens' on developers that might make a development scheme 'unviable'. Thus, policies and planning standards (for example, affordable housing, parking, design, density, open space and so on) embedded in statutory local plans, which had been fully consulted on when they were drawn up, could be abandoned if they made a development scheme 'unviable'.

Finally, and most alarming, it is up to the development industry to define what is financially viable. The measure of viability is defined by the NPPF as 'the competitive return' to the landowner and developer. Thus, in the viability assessment, if developers claim a 20 per cent profit as the 'industry standard' (which is judged by the RICS and the development industry to be the normal level of developer profit), this amount of land value is automatically *not* available for affordable housing, schools funding, infrastructure spending or other planning obligations. Equally, if a landowner demands a further 20–50 per cent for his own profit, planning obligations are reduced even further. Their 'competitive returns' have precedence over the policies in local plans.

There is little opportunity for local authorities or communities to contest the level of competitive returns. Competitive returns are not regarded as 'planning matters' even though they have major planning implications. If housebuilders are ever challenged about the rate of return, their answer is that the rate of return is required by the banks and they have no discretion over this. Yet, these financial conventions have not come out of the blue; rather, they come directly from the finance sector and are agreed with no interrogation by the RICS. Interestingly, there is relatively little research into actual rates of return from development or the justification for finance sector targets. Professor Neil Crosby at the University of Reading, who is an expert in this field, concluded from a survey of the literature on development profits that 'expected returns for property development projects are more opaque than for investment properties and owe more to rules of thumb than to any serious analysis'.[1]

Another RICS argument that the individual circumstances of the developers and landowners should be ignored in viability assessment makes no sense when dealing with corporate landowners or developers (as the Oxford North case study in Chapter 10 shows).

The impact of NPPF viability assessment has been far-reaching. At a stroke, it effectively overruled affordable housing policies in local plans. Furthermore, if communities fought back to defend these policies, the heavy hand of the big property consultancies like Savills, BNP Paribas and CBRE, along with the RICS, and the rest of the property lobby was brought to bear at council planning committees and public inquiries. So-called independent viability reports commissioned by local authorities to check the viability reports submitted by developers are little protection because they are invariably commissioned from the same 'club' of London surveying consultants that rarely probe into industry assumptions and practices.

In viability case after viability case, the hands of local authorities and planning inspectors have been tied by these assessments, lowering the level of affordable housing and other planning obligations. Rose Grayston wrote a report for Shelter in 2017 spelling out in detail the scale of the losses of affordable housing across the country. She found that in one year, 2,500 affordable homes were lost in England because developers were able to exploit the 'viability loophole' (Grayston, 2017). This is a mile away from the NPPF commitment to 'sustainable development'.

Consequently, any community or local government challenge to viability assessment has been an immense struggle. It is David versus Goliath, with the property establishment and the government throwing everything at the objectors. For example, it took six years of campaigning to overthrow the gross injustice of speculative market values being accepted as benchmarks for viability assessments instead of assessing the price of land as a value that takes into account local authority policies requiring a percentage of affordable housing. The former approach hugely reduced the technical viability of schemes while the latter, by reducing land value, made them a lot more viable. In the Parkhurst Road case in 2018, Islington Council was finally able to establish in the High Court that land value in viability assessment should reflect policy obligations, not a speculative market price.[2]

Similarly, local groups in London fought at a series of inquiries and tribunals for the principle that viability assessments prepared by property consultancies for developers and landowners should be published so the public could make up their own mind about the viability of development schemes in their neighbourhood. For them, the use of 'commercial confidentiality' clauses in viability reports was a smokescreen to stop third parties interrogating viability models. The 35 per cent Campaign in Southwark, a residents group campaigning for adherence to council local plan policy of 35 per cent affordable housing in all new developments in their area, and a residents group in Greenwich Peninsula, used Freedom of Information (FOI) requests and appeals to successfully convince the Information Commissioner that the public has a right to viability information under planning law. The judge in the appeal tribunal for Greenwich Peninsula Residents Association concluded that release of viability information was not, in fact, a threat to business competition. When this information was eventually disclosed, it revealed that viability assessments had deliberately underestimated the value and profits from new housing development schemes so that developers and landowners could justify less affordable housing than the local authority required (Mathiason, 2015).

Indeed, it was clear to campaigners that there is a 'viability industry' of consultants who were selling their ability to reduce planning obligations, in other words, to 'game the system'. As a result of legal challenges and further evidence of the viability industry running rings around local authorities and communities, local authorities began to produce their own policy guidance on viability assessment, including clauses that required the regularisation of viability modelling and the full public disclosure of viability assessment reports. Islington Council in London in 2016 was the pioneer in local authority viability guidance. It has already made a difference to the amount of affordable housing negotiated in that borough. Other councils have now followed suit.

Nevertheless, paragraph 173 of the NPPF remained on the statute book until 2018, when a revised NPPF was published – but not before developers and landowners had taken out huge profits from viability assessment throughout the boom of 2012–18. The suggestion made by ministers in 2012 that viability assessment was a temporary 'recession measure' to help the housebuilders over the post-crash period proved to be false because ministers kept the viability clause in place throughout the property boom that followed.

The introduction of a new viability policy and guidance in 2018 and 2019 was an acknowledgement that the infamous paragraph 173 of the 2012 guidance was becoming a scandal. However, neither the HBF nor the RICS wanted to see viability assessment removed, and it was reformulated thus:

> Where up-to-date policies have set out the contributions expected from development, planning applications that comply with them should be assumed to be viable. It is up to the applicant to demonstrate whether particular circumstances justify the need for a viability assessment at the application stage. The weight to be given to a viability assessment is a matter for the decision maker, having regard to all the circumstances in the case, including whether the plan and the viability evidence underpinning it is up to date, and any change in site circumstances since the plan was brought into force. All viability assessments, including any undertaken at the plan-making stage, should reflect the recommended approach in national planning guidance, including standardised inputs, and should be made publicly available. (MHCLG, 2018: para 57)

Under this new policy, each local authority local plan will be 'viability assessed' to determine, in property market viability terms, what is a reasonable level of planning obligation for the plan area, including the affordable housing obligation. Developers are expected to deliver the affordable housing percentage set down in the local plan, but – and it is a big but – if developers claim that they are unable to meet the affordable housing obligation, they can make a case for a reduction using viability assessment. In practice, this looks very much like the paragraph 173 system in another form with a bit more discretion to the local authority. All the limitations of viability assessment and scope for gaming the system remain. In fact, there is new scope for manipulation. Since planning obligations are applied across a large plan area and are intended to prevail for several years across the lifetime of the plan, there will plainly be large variations of development profitability across the plan area and over time – and thus ample scope for developers and landowners to demand viability reassessments and reductions of planning obligations. Developers will claim that local plans are not up to date or that the local plan area viability assessment is inadequate. On top of that, all the old technical questions about the reliability of the RICS guidance on viability kick in yet gain. Issues of competitive returns, variations in input data and difficulties of determining benchmark land values and developer profits have not gone away. The concept of 'standardised inputs' has been introduced but one suspects that it will be the RICS that determines what these inputs will be.

Although the new viability assessment clause contains the concession that viability assessments should be made publicly available, and this is important, how this operates in practice will be critical. Will all the viability information be made available well before the planning application goes to committee so that third parties have an opportunity to analyse it? How much help will planning officers be willing or able to give to objectors?

Unfortunately, despite the vigorous criticism of viability assessment, it is still with us. It is an instrument of a market-centred approach to planning for housing – it is not in any sense community or environment centred. Yet, it is now embedded deep in local plans and in decision-making over most planning applications for new housing. It is a big win for the property lobby.

Conclusion

The property lobby has been extraordinarily successful in bending planning and housing policy in its own direction and to its own advantage. This has been possible because the government has given way with apparent ease. The real losers are local communities who have found that local plan policies for affordable housing mean very little despite their engagement in exhaustive public consultations, and that the government and local authorities appear to buckle under pressure far too easily. Without community protests, it could be much worse. On the other hand, the financial crash of 2008 and its continued reverberations have seemingly cemented the power of the property lobby even more firmly. It is to this issue that we turn in Chapter 7.

7

The 2008 financial crash continues

The 2008 financial crash is still reverberating through the economy and UK politics – and the housing crisis is one of its many casualties. Ten years or more since Lehman Brothers, Northern Rock and HBOS went bankrupt, bringing the financial system crashing down, the economy and politics of the UK are still in shock. The financial crash hit the UK housing market very hard. There was a slump in house prices, a halt to housebuilding and a severe liquidity crisis for the banks. It created economic and political conditions that perpetuated the housing crisis for ten years and more. The implications have spread into every aspect of civic society. In the Brexit debate, the national divide between the haves and have-nots in housing is a key factor in the arguments about how 'left behind' communities feel about Brexit. This chapter explores the implications of the 2008 financial crash and what it means for tackling the housing crisis in the UK.

The financial crash was largely created by reckless lending for property development by US banks and finance groups, which poured money into property in the preceding decade. Bank lending was heavily directed at the housing market above all other parts of the property sector. In the boom, mortgage companies in the US sold mortgages to all comers, with little scrutiny of their ability to pay. As much as 80 per cent of all mortgage loans in the US were 'self-certified' (Farlow, 2013: 41). Investors got in on the act, speculating in portfolios of mortgages including 'sub-prime' or high-risk mortgages taken out by poorer families and by people remortgaging their properties to spend on consumer goods. Hedge funds and other investor groups 'shorted' the housing market, that is, bet against the market recovering, and made billions out of the collapse in prices, in other words, out of the misery of ordinary homeowners (as clinically illustrated in the 2015 film *The big short*). When confidence fell, the portfolios of mortgages that had been wilfully traded on the financial markets were worthless and many families were evicted because they could not afford their mortgage payments.

A similar sequence of events occurred in the UK but with less severity. There was less sub-prime lending and fewer people lost their homes but the contagion from the US banking system spread quickly. UK banks had invested heavily in property during 2000–07: 31 per cent of their investments were in mortgages and 20 per cent were in commercial real estate (only 8 per cent were loans to businesses). High-risk mortgage lending became the norm. Building societies and banks made loans on properties valued at six or seven times the income of homeowners (compared with two or three times in earlier periods). As in the US, many loans were over 100 per cent of the value of the house with very low or no deposits. When the financial crash came, many could not afford the repayments on their homes, which were now worth a lot less and could not be sold. Building societies and banks were in crisis. Northern Rock, which was responsible for 20 per cent of all UK mortgage lending in 2007, had to be rescued by the government in 2008, followed by the nationalisation of the giant HBOS and RBS banks (which had also invested heavily in the US sub-prime market).

Although the financial crash was a disastrous event for housing, the housing market is highly unstable for other reasons as well. As we saw in Chapter 4, land and property, in particular, housing – interest rates, prices, mortgage debt and supply – are at the heart of every economic cycle and every economic crash. Many observers have noted that property speculation and house price inflation are underlying causes of UK economic instability. Farlow, for example, observes that 'crashes are largely a result of asset bubbles in housing' (Farlow, 2013: 29).

Property cycles have been studied in depth by academics and commentators. They are endemic to the UK economy. There is much discussion of their length and frequency. Long cycles of around 18 years and short cycles of four to five years have been postulated by Barras (2009) in his path-breaking work on the subject. He describes a model of the typical building cycle as follows:

> Increasing demand > upward swing in building starts > demand stalls > oversupply of new homes > fall in building starts > falling rents and prices > slump

In this cycle, there is often a credit boom of freely available mortgages as demand rises and building accelerates, then a credit crunch when interest rates rise, demand falls and building grinds to a halt. Sometimes, credit crunches are due to external shocks such as the oil price rise of 1972; often, they are within the national economic system itself. Property cycles can be interpreted as following the general business cycle and the rise and fall in business confidence. However, another explanation is that housing cycles are a primary cause of booms and busts, with a heavy impact on consumer demand and borrowing (Barras, 2009: 73).

There is also a distinct geography to the property cycle. In the boom, money pours into housing and mortgages in high-demand areas of the country like larger cities and London and the South East. Speculative investment targets high-end housing and flats in city centres and waterfronts, pushing up prices throughout the city. Those trying to get on the housing ladder or on waiting lists are priced out. For those already well housed, this is no problem – rising prices makes them better off. However, the gap between those who can afford the new price levels and those who cannot grows sharply, creating both an income and generational divide, and leaving the government split over which side to support – the rising market or those locked out of the market. In high-demand areas, as the boom peaks, house prices fall most sharply from very high levels and new housing sites are mothballed. Many homeowners find themselves in negative equity and, at worst, people lose their homes.

There is a different situation in the low-demand areas of the country. There is less investor interest so that land and housing prices are significantly lower and rise more slowly. However, when the boom surges in London and the South East, there is a ripple of increasing prices across the country. But prices remain relatively low compared with high-demand areas and fall less quickly in the downturn than in high-demand areas.

The UK housing boom of the 2000s, particularly in London as we have seen, was fuelled by international 'safe house' investment and property trading, which pushed up prices in the capital and the wider South East of England to levels that were unaffordable to all but a small segment of the population. Exactly the same cycle took place in the 2014–18 period, when the UK economy moved out of recession but, fuelled by low interest rates and overseas investment, investors poured into London property. Speculators who had bought land and built blocks of luxury flats or high-end houses in the boom faced a sharp collapse in the investment market when the economy slowed down at the end of this period due, in part, to Brexit. The classic case being the luxury Battersea Power Station development, which was bought from the receivers in 2010 by a Malaysian consortium who planned to convert it into 250 luxury flats aimed at overseas buyers, with office space for Apple's headquarters. When the market peaked in 2017 and Brexit fears grew, there was a sudden drop in interest in luxury flats by overseas buyers. Meanwhile, in the North, the Midlands, Scotland

and Wales, prices rose during the same period and continued to do so after the overall market in London had slowed down.

When a crash occurs, the national housing market as a whole is affected. National restrictions on bank lending or rising interest rates affect everybody, and under these circumstances, the large housebuilders gradually withdraw from development across the country. Although there may be some places where demand remains healthy, the corporate message is to withhold investment. The collapse of the market in high-demand areas, especially in London and the South East, pulls every other region down with it. Recovery can take three or four years, as happened after the 1973 crash, the 1992 slump and the 2008 crash. Yet, the people who are most hurt are not the big developers, financial institutions and individual speculators. They ride out the storm with their land banks, personal wealth, long lines of credit and government bail-outs. The real losers are those trying to get onto the housing ladder.

Despite the piles of books and publications written about the 2008 financial crash describing the irresponsibility of the banks and financial institutions, and poor government regulation, it could and probably will happen again. There are well-publicised fears of another crash around the corner due to overvalued housing, mounting mortgage debt, possible interest rate rises and the economic fallout from Brexit. Despite Bank of England rhetoric about tighter lending rules, there are once again concerns about the lowering of lending standards, for example, not insuring loans against default and making it easier for households to buy new homes through Help to Buy.

Why does the UK housing market create boom and bust?

Why is housing so susceptible to boom and bust in the UK and seemingly not so in many European countries, notably, Germany, the Netherlands and Scandinavia? There are four main reasons: first, because so much of the UK economy rests on home ownership and mortgage debt; second, because housing and land prices (in which so much is invested by households and businesses) are so sensitive to interest rates, economic sentiment and household finances; third, because of the inability of the volume housebuilders to respond to increasing demand so that even at a time when borrowing costs are low, there are not enough houses on the market; and, finally, and not to be forgotten, there is poor government regulation of the market – in fact, the government actually celebrates increasing prices and consumer borrowing. As King (2006: 104) put it in his book about homeownership in the 2000s: 'Government encouraged a climate of speculation and risk taking on the part of households and institutions.'

Thus, the ratio of total mortgage debt to gross domestic product (GDP) went from 50 per cent in the early 2000s to 80 per cent by the time of the 2008 financial crash (Farlow, 2013: 32). When the financial crash came, house prices fell by 20 per cent between July 2007 and January 2009, instantly depressing demand and development. It is this level of volatility that is so damaging to the UK economy. In focusing so much attention on mortgage debt and house prices – on the up and downs of the homeowners' market – policymakers are diverted away from considering those who cannot get into this market and need social and affordable housing.

The bail-out

The financial crash and the recession that followed were traumatic for the government. Not only did the market slump send the banks, landowners, developers and landlords into shock mode, but government tax revenues fell. The government leapt into radical interventions. It bailed out the banks and the developers – in effect, a bail-out to cover bad housing market loans. It ignored the homeless, social housing and the low paid – and, in fact, made their grave situation very much worse by targeting government help on the financial institutions and the developers, giving next to nothing to bail out to those in housing need.

The immediate consequence was that the housing market stalled for three to four years, led by London and the South East, which had been the main beneficiary of the bail-out, only picking up in 2013. As in other cycles, 'wild optimism was followed by deep pessimism' (King, 2010: 83). While the banks' money taps had been wide open throughout the 2000s, they tightened up their lending rules so that demand for market homes dried up, especially from those on low to medium incomes, who had already been hit by rising unemployment and flatlining wages.

The collapse was also an opportunity. The housebuilders cut back on their existing projects but took advantage of falling land prices to replenish their land banks. Even in these straightened times, they were able to borrow to buy land at knock-down prices ready for the next upswing, knowing that they would be able to benefit from the increase in land prices as the cycle moved out of recession (Payne, 2015). They could not lose. Foolishly, the government itself did not buy land in the downturn; instead, it ordered a fire sale of its own land and properties to get money into the Treasury. The bail-out was not just a lifeboat for the banks and finance houses. The government pumped money into the land and property market through QE, Help to Buy and a range of grants, subsidies and tax breaks to volume builders. It was short-term panic instead of long-term thinking – and those waiting to get on the housing ladder were made to suffer even longer.

Scapegoating town planning

Then, as if to hide this corporate welfare, the Coalition government turned its fire not onto the banks or the developers, but perversely onto the town planners in local government. The planners were accused by the Chancellor of the Exchequer, no less, of causing the housing crisis by holding up development and placing undue restrictions on developers. Therefore, in significant reforms to the plan-led planning system, local councils would be 'forced' to build new homes even if they were opposed to development (Dominiczak, 2015).

Planners in local government – who, in reality, have little power over whether landowners sell or builders build – became the scapegoats for market failure; hence the issuing of the developer-friendly NPPF in 2012, and the 'presumption in favour of sustainable development', as if that in itself would increase the number of new homes. Of course, as anyone who looked at a property magazine would know, the housebuilders had thousands of planning permissions at their disposal, and their decision to build had nothing to with the planners and everything to do with their business model. The Coalition government found it more politically convenient to blame the planners than to own up to the failures of its allies in the property industry and its own failure to regulate the market properly.

Austerity as bail-out

The longer-term impact on public spending on social and affordable housing was equally significant. The recession was used by the government as a justification for a decade-long reduction in public spending, which, of course, made the recession worse and more prolonged. This austerity decade was particularly severe on all those parts of the public sector that deal with housing, for example, social housing expenditure, health services, town planning, local government services, public transport, social care and social welfare. A cap was placed on borrowing by local authorities that halted public housebuilding programmes, and there were massive cuts to their annual revenue grants (up to 45 per cent) that severely reduced public services, including support for voluntary sector help for the homeless and mentally ill. Affordable housing grants were limited and finally halted, the bedroom tax was introduced and Right to Buy was extended – a catalogue of disasters that created a new housing crisis.

In other words, not only was the front-line support structure for social housing and the homeless starved of funds, but local councils were unable to borrow money to build homes or control private sector rents. Local authorities were pressurised by the government to sell off their land and housing estates to developers, and many did so because they were unable to undertake estate regeneration and development themselves. Some local authorities, instead of holding onto their land or thinking creatively with their local communities about what they might do, willingly joined in, selling off whole estates and tracts of building land to developers for a song despite angry community protests (Watt, forthcoming).

A notable example in London is the sale by Labour-controlled Southwark Council in 2013 of the Heygate Estate to Lendlease, a giant Australian development company. It was sold for a mere £50 million when it was previously valued at £150 million. Covering 9 hectares, the Heygate comprised 1,214 flats almost all of which were social housing. The council spent £44 million on decanting the residents and then granted permission to Lendlease for 2,535 new apartments, of which only 79 were social housing. The *Metro* (White, 2017) newspaper reported that marketing began in Singapore and all 51 flats in the first phase of the development were sold by Lendlease to overseas investors at prices between £750,000 and £1.5 million. The council policy for 35 per cent affordable housing was ignored.[1]

For Southwark Council this was a panic land sale and a panic planning consent triggered, in part, by the financial crash and the fear that no development would take place unless the Council took drastic action. The council tore up its own plans in the process. In this way, the financial crash and the recession, rather than being a sombre lesson in how not to manage the property market and the housing crisis, became the justification for national policies (and many local decisions) that made the housing crisis worse.

Conclusion

The 2008 financial crash was not just another moment in recent history from which we have all now moved on. On the contrary, it is still very much with us in the way that the property market has been able to re-establish its dominance over our lives, and in the way that local government has caved in to market pressures. The government has turned the tables on communities by backing austerity and the very sector of the economy – the finance/property market – that created the crisis in the first place, at the same time as stigmatising social and affordable housing. While the volume housebuilding sector was pampered, the public housing sector and not-for-profit housing sectors that could actually make a difference to those in housing need were given only crumbs.

The financial crash and the austerity years that followed were not inevitable or unavoidable; they were a political choice. The government response to the property crash and the housing crisis was driven largely by ideology. It refused to take into account the numerous studies of the housing market that have stressed its speculative nature and the necessity for the government to build homes for those in need. The ideology that the market knows best was reinforced by the property lobby that placed its own interests at the top of the minds of the government. Immediately after the financial crash and throughout the years that followed, the property lobby was at the government's door saying: 'If you want new housing to be built, we must be rescued, for without us, there will be no recovery and your targets for housebuilding will not be met, and the crisis will get worse'. The government accepted this argument because it believed that the private market was the solution – and, bluntly, because the housebuilders, financiers and landowners were their friends.

The property lobby and the government were, and still are, mutually indispensable. In Chapter 8, we look in more detail at how this ideology plays out in the housebuilding sector, shaping the way that it responds to the national need for social and affordable housing.

8

The housebuilders and affordable housing

The question that has dogged the politics of planning and housing in the UK for the last 40 years is this: since landowners and developers are sweeping up large windfalls from developing land for housing, how much should they put back in planning obligations to provide affordable housing? As the government has repeatedly ducked its own responsibility since the 1980s for funding new affordable housing, or for taxing windfall gains, local authorities and communities are engaged in a continuous battle with landowners and developers, contesting levels of affordable housing on a site-by-site basis. Communities quite rightly say that they are directly affected by new developments and a decent amount of the windfall should go back to those most affected. Local authorities want to maximise the percentage of affordable housing on housing sites, while developers want to minimise it – and developers spend millions on consultants and lawyers to ensure that they get what they want.

The scale of the windfall is staggering. A planning consent on a piece of agricultural land in South East England can raise its price at least 100 times without a brick being laid. For example, a site worth £45,000 as agricultural land can be sold for £4.5 million with planning consent for housing. It has been estimated that across much of the country, at least a half of the price of a house is the land cost, so that in 2014/15, for example landowners obtained £9 billion in profit from land they sold for housing in England, in other words, an average of £60,000 per house. This figure went up to £13 billion in 2016–17 (Aubrey, 2018). Imagine how many affordable homes could be built if just 50 per cent of this land value increase was captured by local authorities? It would amount to £6.5 billion a year for public services and better housing.

The battle over planning obligations

Planning obligations have been part of the planning system for the past 50 years. Section 52 agreements or planning gain were included in the Town and Country Planning Act 1971, and renamed 'planning obligations' in Section 106 of the Town and Country Planning Act

1990. All local planning authorities of all political persuasions include policies of planning obligations in their local plans. In addition, the CIL (Community Infrastructure Levy), introduced in the Planning Act 2008, applies infrastructure charges to new developments to fund infrastructure works such as opening up sites for development by land remediation or road access across the district. Not that anyone is happy with this system: developers and landowners regard CIL as a tax on development; while local authorities say that CIL falls well short of the amount required to fund the social and physical infrastructure needed for housing and commercial development. In the event, many local authorities do not yet have approved schedules of CIL charges. Strangely, CIL cannot be used to pay for affordable housing – only Section 106 can do that. This misses a trick because affordable housing is surely an essential form of infrastructure in a good planning scheme and Section 106 on its own is simply inadequate as a funding mechanism for affordable housing.

Planning obligations required by local authorities range from road improvements, to contributions to new school buildings, construction skills training and new open spaces, each tailored to the specific circumstances of the development proposed. The most contentious obligation by far is the amount of affordable housing required by a local authority. The reason for this is that affordable housing reduces land value, while other contributions actually increase value by making the housing scheme more attractive to buyers. Moreover, from the developers' point of view, affordable homes make adjoining market homes less desirable, lowering their prices and making them more difficult to sell. Thus, land value is depressed where local authorities state firmly that their policies on affordable housing will be applied to housing development land. Put simply, affordable housing land is worth less than market housing land. This difference in value is the central contention in the long-running dispute between landowners/developers and local authorities/communities over planning gain (Monk et al, 2005: 185–208).

Take the aforementioned example of the greenfield site worth £45,000 for agricultural use but £4.5 million after obtaining planning permission for 20 new homes. If the developer was required by the local authority to provide 50 per cent of the new housing as genuinely affordable housing (ten units), this could reduce the land value to £2.5 million, a loss of a £2 million windfall profit to the landowner – though still a tidy windfall gain on the land alone of nearly £2.5 million without a brick being laid. If the local authority is unwilling or unable to put an affordable housing obligation in place because they are intimidated by the allegation that they have cut the landowner profit by half, the community faces a loss of ten affordable homes. How can this be acceptable in the context of a severe national shortage of affordable housing?

As suggested earlier, developers do not usually object to planning obligations that require funding for 'hard' infrastructure like road access or land remediation because these measures help to open up their sites and increase value. Nor do they object to providing funding for new school buildings since a new primary school near the site makes new homes attractive to prospective buyers. In fact, without a guarantee of school places nearby, many developers would not go ahead in the first place. When it comes to 'soft' infrastructure such as funding for affordable housing, bus routes, GP surgeries or community centres, housebuilders see these items as not creating value and not their responsibility.

Thus, amid all the claims from the property lobby about the slowness of the planners in processing their planning applications, the fact is that negotiation inevitably takes a long time because developers fiercely contest the planning obligations required in local plans every step of the way. At the root of these negotiations is very often the effect of affordable housing obligations on land value and profits. Developers and landowners want to maximise the number of private housing units on their sites. More than that, they want to capture the increase in value over time. If a local authority demands more affordable housing, developers will try to increase the density of the development to pay for the affordable housing. Equally, cash-strapped local authorities may want more development on site to enable more funding for neighbourhood services. There is always pressure to get more development on site to maximise development value and provide sufficient funds for infrastructure and planning obligations.

An interesting study of a major development scheme in West London on the site of the Old Oak Common rail yard demonstrates just this dilemma. Robinson and Attuyer (2019) describe how developers and a mayoral development corporation were involved in prolonged negotiations about the level of value than could be 'extracted' from the site to meet both developer and public requirements. They found that public authorities wanted densities to go up so that they could extract more planning gain for costly infrastructure works and, by putting more development on site, can meet government housing targets. The developers, on the other hand, wanted to maximise the percentage of private housing but pushed back on higher densities and affordable housing because for the sort of private housing that they want to sell, they preferred lower densities. Hence, good design and high-quality place making are at the mercy of intricate arguments over how much development value a scheme can generate.

This contested model of cross-subsidy is why the outcomes of the planning system please no one. How much better it would be if Old Oak Common was owned publicly, reclaimed with government money and then developed by a public–civic partnership, putting the aims of quality place making and balanced communities first, rather than inserting them on the basis of what the developers can afford or the planning authority can extract in planning gain. The principle of master planning that was the foundation of the new towns and many contemporary developments in the Netherlands, Scandinavia and Germany has gone out of the window.

How much appreciation in land value is captured by planning obligations? In one study, Bentley (2016) estimates that CIL and Section 106 capture 27 per cent of value appreciation from residential land development. Although this means that 73 per cent of value appreciation goes to the landowner and developer, which is a massive windfall, the truth is that this is likely to be a significant underestimate because it omits the loss of value over time. For example, the windfall over the lifetime of major transport schemes such as Crossrail, motorways or transport hubs that appreciate value to surrounding sites over a long period of time is likely to be much higher than 73 per cent. The Jubilee Line extension from Central London to Canary Wharf cost £3.5 billion to build, and in the ten years from 1992 to 2002, this project created an uplift of more than £13 billion for landowners in the vicinity of the 11 new stations. None of this uplift was captured by the community.[1] Similarly, large housing schemes may take 20 years to build out but the Section 106 and CIL capture will normally take place only at the time of the planning consent.

Planning obligations policies should aim to capture some of this uplift over time and many local authorities attempt to do this by inserting 'overage' clauses in planning obligations contracts. Overage is a payment from the developer or landowner if and when certain conditions such as sales from housing or the completion of phases of the development have been reached. Overage clauses, sometimes called Review Mechanisms, thus attempt to claw back some of the speculative gain in value from long term development projects. They address the reality that development is about long term value growth – and community/local authorities have every right to claim some of this back. Nevertheless, whether review mechanisms are in operation or not, in my estimation, barely 5 per cent of the land value created by development in England is captured by Planning Obligations.

Speculation in land

The real profit from housing development comes from speculation in land. The developer will pay a price for land (or buy an option) based on the value of the land with the expectation of planning permission, but he will aim to sell houses based on the expectation that the value of the land will appreciate from the time of acquisition. This gives him a straight profit: the difference between the purchase price for the land plus construction costs and the eventual sales prices of the houses. Any planning obligation required by the local authority will reduce this profit. Therefore, part of the bet on the land price will be estimating the level of planning obligations that he can negotiate with the local authority. If he can buy land based on one level of planning obligations but then negotiate this level down later, he has made a useful profit on the land purchase. For example, if a large site is bought for 500 housing units expecting a ten-year build-out period, the value of the site is the value based on house prices and planning obligations when the land was acquired. However, if house prices rise by, say, 10 per cent over the ten-year period (which is not unusual) and planning obligations can be negotiated down over the lifetime of the project, the increased value will be captured by the developer. He may share some of this speculative profit with the landowner – but how much does the community get?

Of course, it is possible that if a developer overpays for land believing that he can ignore or negotiate down the planning obligations required, he will often try later to argue that planning obligations should be proportionate to the original price paid for the land. In a landmark planning case in Clay Farm, Cambridgeshire, in 2010, when the developer of 2,300 homes, Countryside Properties, said that it could not provide the 40 per cent affordable housing required because of the price it paid for the land, the Secretary of State ruled against the company, saying that the delivery of planning obligations should not rely on the price paid for the land. If the developer had overpaid because he had not taken the local authority planning obligations policy seriously when he negotiated the land price with the landowner, then that was their problem. A review of legal decisions on housing affordability and planning gain in 2010 concluded that 'it is not the role of the planning system to protect historic land values or protect developers and landowners from bad decisions' (Young and Balch, 2010). As we noted Chapter 6 on viability assessment, this same conclusion was reached in the Parkhurst Road case in Islington in 2018.

It is important to realise that planning obligations do not mean that landowners and developers actually suffer any loss from the development of the affordable housing required by a planning obligation. They discharge their obligation by selling their homes to a housing association. Until 2015, housing associations were eligible for social housing grants or affordable housing grants, which enabled them to buy homes off developers. In effect, the developer is paid from the public purse to meet their affordable housing obligations. The developer's contribution is limited to the reduced price that they sell the 'affordable units' to the housing association for compared with the price if they were sold as market homes. This 'affordable homes' price is often not much less than the price of market homes and, in some cases, may be more because they can be sold en bloc with no marketing or drip-feeding required. In reality, therefore, honouring the planning obligation is not much of a sacrifice.

Developer resistance to tenure mix

The contention over affordable housing obligations is not just with the number of affordable units required by a local authority; it is also with the type and distribution of affordable housing across a new housing site. One of the primary objectives of good planning across the country is to resist single-tenure housing schemes on large housing sites and to insist on 'mixed-tenure' development. Mixed tenure, that is, a mixture of private, public, rented and for-sale units across a housing site, is intended to meet a wide range of housing needs, reduce social stigma and enhance 'community cohesion'. The background to this requirement is that many planners believe that social class divisions are reinforced by the physical separation of private housing and rented housing.

One of the most notorious cases of physical separation is the Cutteslowe walls in Oxford. In this development, a physical wall separated a council housing scheme from an adjoining private housing development. Both housing schemes were built at the same time in the 1930s. A wall was erected between the two housing areas in 1934 by the developer of the private housing. Through roads that had previously crossed the Cutteslowe area were divided in half and given different street names for the public and private parts of the street. There were no gates or passageways through the wall to permit the movement of the residents of the rented housing through the private housing. Despite years of protests by the residents of the council estate, the developer refused to knock down the wall. It was finally demolished by the council in 1959, 25 years after it was built (Collison, 1963).

Housing class divisions are not simply about social class and stigma; they are also about race and culture. In 1967, a path-breaking research paper by Rex and Moore (1967) documenting racial housing divisions in Sparkbrook in Birmingham drew attention to the de facto segregation of housing markets in many UK inner cities. Little has changed since (Harrison et al, 2005). A landmark ICM survey of racism in Britain in 2018 revealed widespread discrimination in employment, leisure, law enforcement and housing. This survey showed that homeownership among minority ethnic groups fell by ten percentage points between 2001 and 2016, compared with 4 per cent for white people; and white people have disproportionately been able to take advantage of Right to Buy compared with minority ethnic households. Consequently, almost half of black families are concentrated in what little council housing the country has left, and one in five are in private rental accommodation and 36 per cent of homeless people are from ethnic minority backgrounds (Gulliver, 2017). Moreover, black and minority ethnic housing associations claim that the government does not recognise these disparities in the housing system and should allocate housing funds specifically for this sector.

From a town planning perspective the Sparkbrook study led to the adoption by local authorities of mixed-tenure policies in local plans. Yet despite this established practice, social and racial divisions continue to have a powerful effect on the layout of new housing schemes. Developers and landowners, always driven by price and value, are highly sensitive to the impact of mixed tenure and social mix on house prices. When a new housing scheme is being designed with local authority planners, housebuilders will invariably try to persuade the planners to locate affordable or social housing away from the private units, often in the less desirable parts of the site. Planners may demand the 'pepper-potting' of private and social units across a new estate so that you are unable to tell the difference between new units on the basis of tenure. In spite of this best practice guidance, housebuilders often succeed in separating tenure types so that there are evident physical housing class divisions in many new volume housing developments. Housing for social rent invariably ends up in the worst locations.

For example, take an urban extension developed by English Partnerships in partnership with private developers at Upton on the edge of Northampton. This scheme, comprising 1,350 new homes, was a government pathfinder in sustainable urban extensions in the 2000s. It was designed with extensive community consultation and included a range of sustainable design measures, including Sustainable Urban Drainage (SUDS) and low-carbon homes. Yet, the affordable housing element is distinguished by more cramped, lower-quality development, lower specifications internally and externally, and less car parking provision, and is located in a less attractive part of the development next to an existing housing scheme from which it is separated by a wall. Thus, even where, as in this case, the landowner was a government agency and there was detailed consultation on all aspects of the scheme, the developers were able to insist that the affordable housing was of lower specification and located away from most of the market housing and greenfield open space.

Another example of housing class divisions is the huge Greenwich Peninsula housing development in South East London. The plan was for 10,000 houses and flats on land previously owned (and reclaimed) by English Partnerships. It was sold to an overseas company in 2013 at a bargain price of £50 million, and attracted £50 million of affordable housing grants. Despite this preferential treatment for the developer and new landowner, the planners at the London borough of Greenwich agreed to accept the developers' claim that their scheme would not be viable if they were required to meet the local authority planning obligation figure of 35 per cent affordable housing. Then, they agreed that the prime riverside sites overlooking Canary Wharf on the north bank of the Thames would be reserved for upmarket private flats while the affordable and social housing would be at the back of the site away from the riverside (and closest to major roads and industry). This layout was described as 'social cleansing' by local residents (Kitson, 2014).

Why local authorities give in

Why do local authorities give in so meekly even when they have policies on affordable housing and mixed development in their local plans? The answer is that they are under intense pressure from the government to meet housing targets, and they are poorly prepared politically and technically to deal with developers who have deep pockets and good connections. The costs of fighting a planning appeal are not small change. Housebuilders, individually or through the HBF, are expert at making their case against 'onerous' planning obligations at local plan examinations, at planning appeals and inquiries, and directly to ministers. They demand lower percentages of affordable housing and flexibility over definitions of affordable housing and the configuration of site layouts. They claim that if planning obligations are too onerous, their schemes will not be viable, and they may claim that they will walk away and the site will remain derelict, or that local authorities will get less if economic conditions deteriorate.

There is a lot at stake for local communities in the battle over planning obligations. With cuts in the direct provision of council housing and private rents going through the roof, communities are reliant on planning obligations to provide new affordable housing. Yet, the crucial negotiations about the details of planning obligations on individual sites between the local authority and the planning applicants are often kept confidential. Even contractual or planning agreements may not be made available to backbench councillors. Yet, it is only by examining the detailed package of planning obligations (and being able to compare this with local plan policy requirements) that communities can judge whether their needs or representations are being taken seriously.

There are always promises of community spin-offs by local authorities and developers when consultation on a new development proposal begins, but trust quickly breaks down when it becomes clear that new facilities such as health centres or social housing come at the bottom of the list of the development when building starts. Some of the spin-offs may not start on site until years later, if at all. Others, such as playgrounds or open space, may be identified as for the community as a whole, but when the homes are built, they are managed as for the exclusive use of the private housing residents. Grant and Mohdin (2019) highlighted a case of a site in Lambeth, South London, where children from a social housing block were not allowed to play in an adjoining play area attached to new private flats even though this had been the agreement with the developer when the private flats were built. This was described by residents as 'segregation'.

Sometimes, the promises made by the developers and local authorities are not actually in their gift, for example, new health centres, employment services or bus routes that require funding and approval or forward planning by other agencies. A typical promise is that there will be neighbourhood shops on a new housing estate. This is easy to say but this promise cannot be delivered by either a developer or a local authority; it will depend on whether there is a willing retailer prepared to set up in the retail shell built by the developer. Thus, in new estates, there are often no corner shops to be seen for many years. Local authorities and developers invariably make promises about the attraction of new developments that they cannot meet. A cynic would say that the promises are made to keep local objectors quiet; others would say that local authorities do not have the negotiating skills or political will to get what they consider the community needs.

Loopholes and get-out clauses

It does not help that contracts about planning obligations are themselves riddled with loopholes and get-out clauses. It is normal for developers and their consultants to try to whittle down the percentages of affordable housing on viability grounds, but the definition of affordable housing has been stretched (as we have seen) to include a range of sub-market products, such as equity share, 'starter homes', discounted homeownership housing, intermediate rent or Build to Rent, which are not affordable to most people on housing waiting lists. The government definition of 'affordable' as 80 per cent of market rent is well above what most people in housing need can afford, or are able to claim from the local housing allowance.

Another indignity of this process is that if any social housing units are finally negotiated, they may be subject to the Right to Buy, and thus do not contribute to the long-term stock of social housing. Even community land trusts and any other social housing bodies receiving grants from local authorities and the government are fighting for the right to be exempt from the Right to Buy.[2] What is the point of a decades-long struggle to build housing that local people need through a community-led housing project if, when the houses are built, the new lovingly designed and built homes can be sold through the Right to Buy?

Usefully for the volume housebuilders and their backers, the value of an affordable home defined in government parlance is significantly higher than a social housing home. Affordable homes may be rented at 80 per cent of market value, while a social housing home is likely to be rented at 30–40 per cent of market value. With this definition, developers and landowners retain a lot of land value if they agree to build 'affordable homes' instead of social housing. This is partly why the number of social housing units negotiated nationally through planning obligations is so tiny. I estimate an average of around 10 per cent on large schemes. A further loophole is to permit 'off-site' or 'commuted sum' payments instead of on-site affordable housing. This avoids the need for on-site mixed-tenure development and protects landowner/developer land value.

Affordable housing obligations have failed

Thus, while, at first sight, it is encouraging that councils require affordable housing in large developments, closer examination reveals an alarming gap between policy and delivery. Most local authorities require on-site affordable housing obligations ranging from 10–40 per cent, yet actual delivery on site is usually well below 20 per cent across most of the country (Brownill et al, 2015). A study in Northamptonshire suggested that the actual level of delivery of affordable housing on site in that region was in the order of 11 per cent (Cochrane et al, 2015). The GLA reported that between 2011 and 2016, developer contributions to affordable housing across London was less than 10 per cent of all affordable homes built in that period.

Most local authorities say that developers do not meet their affordable housing obligations and, in fact, the majority of local authorities do not expect them to do so. A survey by the TCPA of 120 local authorities in 2018 found that despite the fact that 70 per cent of authorities rely on developers to deliver affordable housing through planning obligations, only 2 per cent of authorities were able to achieve their planning obligations for affordable housing 'all of the time' (TCPA, 2018a). Planning obligations policies for affordable housing are plainly not working.

This explains why affordable housing contributions capture only a tiny fraction of the total land value uplift from development. The planning contributions made by the big landowners and developers are so small that they barely register on their balance sheets; their profits soared in recent years in spite of the planning obligations that they complained so much about. The millions that they throw at planning consultants, lawyers and public relations companies into lobbying authorities and ministers to reduce affordable housing obligations have paid off handsomely – but not for those in housing need.

Conclusion

Affordable housing obligations are one of the most contentious battlegrounds between planners and the property market. Affordable housing lowers land value and is fiercely contested by the development sector, particularly if this means providing social housing. The sector has been remarkably successful at obtaining exemptions from and exceptions to affordable housing obligations. Flexible definitions of affordable housing, viability assessment of obligations and variations to mixed development policies have all gone their way.

Local authorities and housing associations have been forced onto the defensive by a succession of government policies aimed at helping out the development sector after the financial crash. Viability assessment of planning obligations and housing targets (with threats of delivery penalties) imposed on local authorities have severely reduced the leverage of local authorities in negotiations – and have increased the risk they will lose costly planning appeals. The Right to Buy has continued to bite into the social housing stock. On top of this, there is a huge inequality in resources between the property sector and local authorities and communities, which is apparent for all to see at planning committee meetings, planning appeals and local plan examinations.

The result is that most of the increase in land values over the past 30 years of booming housing markets has been pocketed by the property sector, with only a fraction channelled into the community or into affordable housing. Planning obligations policies for affordable housing have singularly failed to deliver on the affordable or social housing that the country needs. Government reliance on this mechanism has been misguided and is a cynical cover-up for its close relationship with finance and property market interests.

The planning obligations saga demonstrates that the noble intention of successive governments that the market in land and property can provide affordable housing by a 'trickle-down' or cross-subsidy process is a contradiction in terms. The housing market is not in business to build social or affordable housing. The existence of planning obligations in government planning guidance does little to change this – in fact, it merely highlights the impossibility of making this idea work. The bottom line for landowners and developers is that affordable housing reduces land value; hence, expecting the property market to deliver any significant amount of affordable housing as a planning obligation is doomed to failure. Even during the boom times, it does not deliver, and when the market slumps, developers demand the immediate lowering of planning obligations.

The inevitable conclusion is that relying on the market to help out with the housing crisis is a profound error. It would take monumental political will and technical skill to squeeze any significant increase in affordable housing obligations out of housebuilders and landowners using this approach. Even a radical rebalancing of power in the UK planning system will not get developers to deliver the social and affordable housing that we need. We have reached an impasse.

Before the government started to rely upon planning obligations, building social or affordable housing was the responsibility of councils and housing associations. They were able to do this because they were directly funded by the government, but when the government turned off the taps beginning in the 1980s, councils and housing associations looked for other ways to provide social housing – and, indeed, many began to radically change their objectives away from being providers of social housing. Chapter 9 explores the gradual incorporation of councils and housing associations into the finance–housebuilding complex – and the implications for tackling the housing crisis.

9

How the social and affordable housing sectors got swallowed

In 2015, residents of the Aylesbury Estate in London were faced with plans by Southwark Council to demolish their estate of 2,700 social rented council homes. The council entered into a partnership with Notting Hill Housing Trust, a well-known housing association with a distinguished 50-year record of building homes for social rent in London. However, the partnership entailed building a new estate of 3,500 homes, of which 50 per cent would be homes for sale and only one third would be for social rent. It would lead to a net loss of approximately 1,400 units and the displacement of local residents across the borough and elsewhere. It caused an uproar in the community, who strongly opposed the CPO of their estate. Nonetheless, the inspector at the CPO inquiry in 2018 approved the CPO and the rebuilding project is now going ahead (Minton, 2017).

Notting Hill Housing Trust was formed in 1963 with a mission to build social housing. It had an excellent reputation in London as a housing charity committed to the social housing sector. It now has a stock of 55,000 homes in London. In 2018, it merged with Genesis HA to become Notting Hill Genesis. How could Notting Hill Housing Trust, an association built on values of concern to house the poor and needy of West London, have found itself in the position of going into partnership with a local authority to knock down a council housing estate and replace it with 50 per cent private housing and only 30 per cent social housing? Equally shocking is that a Labour council with one of the largest housing waiting lists in London came to the conclusion that it should demolish an estate of social homes and become a developer for 1,750 private homes at prices well out of reach of people on the waiting list.

In North London, Hackney Council went into partnership with Berkeley Homes to decant 2,000 social housing units and undertake the regeneration of the Woodberry Down Estate, building a total of 5,500 new homes, of which most would be for sale. Indeed, the scheme includes luxury flats of £1 million overlooking a reservoir. As we saw in Chapter 3, Berkeley Homes is an avowed upmarket housing developer whose chairman, Tony Pidgley, has made a personal fortune from such schemes.

How is it that local authorities with huge housing waiting lists have agreed with apparent eagerness to sell their land and housing at bargain-basement prices and permit hundreds of high-priced units that their own residents have little chance of owning? Why have councils become indistinguishable from private developers and landowners, outsourcing development to companies that are making huge profits from council-owned land at the expense of local residents? Why are housing associations becoming like private developers too, using the same development models and exchanging personnel and expertise?

This is not unusual – it is all too common. Anna Minton refers to a report by the London Assembly that identifies 50 estates in London that are undergoing estate regeneration. It is not just a London phenomenon; it is happening all over the country. There are exceptions where councils or housing associations have stood their ground, and some community protests have blunted the worst effects, but this is the trend. We have already seen how financialisation is overwhelming the world of housing policy in a general sense, prioritising market values and prices over social need and the environment. It is now inside the door of the providers of social housing and beginning to eat away at the heart of social housing.

The main reason that this has happened is that funding for social and affordable housing that used to come from the government has been cut back severely over a number of years. Grants have been reduced, not because waiting lists are coming down, but for purely ideological reasons to cut back the powers of local government and force people into homeownership, whether they can afford it or not. Councils faced with a long-term squeeze on their revenue grant from the government are looking at anything and everything to find new sources of income. Housing associations have also had their funding reduced. Hence, many councils and housing associations have responded by effectively becoming property speculators, arguing that unless they can generate profits from commercial housing, they will be unable to fund social and affordable housing and other services. Council officers are being sent out to look for development deals with banks, developers and investors, using council land and money as leverage. This has been rightly termed 'financialised urban entrepreneurialism' (Beswick and Penny, 2018). It includes councils setting up special purpose vehicles (SPVs), comprising private investors, developers and council officials, to undertake development projects. The SPVs act like private companies, with proceedings dealt with on a confidential basis. The idea is that the profits from development, usually expected to be a minimum of 20 per cent, are split between the investors and the council.

Many other local authorities are setting up similar SPVs but this has not been without local controversy because of the implications for existing tenants and the secrecy surrounding these arrangements. In Haringey in North London, the council was forced to withdraw from a proposed SPV because of local outcry. It had planned to go into partnership with Lendlease, the Australian property company that, as we have seen, was already involved in a highly controversial partnership with Southwark Council over the development of the council-owned Heygate Estate. The Haringey SPV would have demolished much of the Northumberland Park Estate located near the Spurs football ground and would have led to the development of 6,400 homes, many of them private flats for sale in the area and across the borough. In return, the council would obtain a share of the profits to build council housing, but at a much lower number than those to be demolished. The council claimed that it would lose £20 million in investment if the joint venture was scrapped. However, because many council homes would be lost in the process, combined with fears that the SPV would not be properly accountable to local people, in July 2018, the council voted not to go ahead with the SPV (*BBC News*, 2018).

To a large extent, the risks of this strategy are not in the hands of councils, housing associations or the community; they depend on the national and local land and property markets. Councils are throwing themselves into the property development marketplace, competing with each other and with other development consortiums for private investors. There are inevitable winners and losers – not all councils can succeed and not all land will achieve the right level of market value to make a profit to house their own people. Under these circumstances, the provision of social and affordable housing becomes a postcode lottery, dependent on the ups and downs of the local and national variations of the property market. The right to decent housing has disappeared. It is no longer a universal 'right' like the right to health or education or social services, nor is it a service directly funded by the government as a national necessity, like roads or the military. It has become a by-product of commercial property ventures and the level of profit that the council can extract from these ventures.

Moreover, the social homes themselves become an investment, part of a commercial value calculation on the balance sheet. Councils and developers calculate the financial value of social and affordable units, and, on this basis, how many can be built and at what rent – naturally, after the 20 per cent profit has been secured by the developer.

Commercial viability and development profit becomes everything. All the partners – the investors, developers, property agents and builders, as well as the council – will want their share. The profit slices come first; the social housing tenant comes last. This is a new financialised form of social housing. As such, every aspect of social housing – rents, tenancy conditions and leases – which were formerly based on the needs of the tenants, are part of the commercial contract with the developer and investor.

This form of housing development leads to a serious breakdown of trust between communities and councils/social landlords. Once councils and housing associations start setting up private companies from which the public is excluded and whose proceedings are deemed confidential, or are published in redacted form, the public quickly loses faith in their representatives and in council officers, who are seen as serving the aims and objectives of the development company, not the public.

As an example, the 35 per cent campaign, a social housing group, reported on a Southwark Council–British Land partnership agreement for 3,000 homes on 46 acres of council-owned land at Canada Water. The campaign asked for a copy of the partnership agreement but was initially told that it was confidential. When it was eventually released, the financial and viability information, including details on affordable housing, public open space agreements and developers' profit share, was redacted.[1] How can redactions of this kind encourage trust between communities and councils? Yet, this approach to confidentiality is not at all unusual. Indeed, as more and more councils enter into deals with developers, the refusal to publish information or redaction of key facts is the answer that the public will get. The consequence is that even if the partnership company states that it has an overarching public service objective, this purpose will be viewed with scepticism by the public if they see that the outcome is, first of all, a blanket of confidentiality. Later, when large blocks of private flats and only a minimum of genuinely affordable housing come out of the ground on publicly owned land, they will view it with anger. From a democratic point of view, these SPVs are counterproductive and feed the alienation of already disadvantaged communities.

The tragedy is that rather than protesting and saying 'no' to this encroachment of financialisation, the bodies that are supposed to stand up for affordable housing – councils and housing associations – are embracing it, often with enthusiasm. Many councils and housing associations have become addicted to growth models and to profit margins, often turning a blind eye to the ethics of their commercial partners. Offshore funds or rapacious developers are all potential partners if they can return the share of profit that the council needs. Councils and housing associations are entering a murky world. How much due diligence is undertaken and is the public allowed to see the due diligence reports?

Once enmeshed in the finance sector, including borrowing from banks, private equity and offshore funds offering affordable housing packages, or raising bonds on the money markets, many councils and housing associations are sucked into ventures that undermine their own social purpose and put their own tenants at risk. Housing associations are now constructing, with the help of city law firms, complex financial vehicles to develop new homes so that the associations are barely recognisable as charitable housing bodies. For example, in 2019 there was a report that one of the larger housing associations, Clarion Housing Association, in 2017/18 built 1,038 'affordable' sale homes at 80 per cent of the market rate and just 31 social rent homes. Elsewhere, A2Dominion housing association are building flats for sale at £500,000 to £1 million in fashionable Shoreditch in London and up to £2 million each in Vauxhall (Jones, 2019).

This in the context in which the finance sector, once wary of the social and affordable housing sector, has turned around its perspective on housing investment. Private finance groups are offering substantial loans to housing associations to build social housing because with the right mix of 'affordable housing', banks can made a tidy profit. Housing associations borrow £6 billion a year from the private sector, with 80 per cent from banks and building societies.[2] A review of headlines in housing journals gives a flavour of the headlong rush of housing associations into the arms of private capital – and of private capital into the social housing sector:

- Large housing association borrows £175 million from North American investors (*Inside Housing*, 17 January 2019)
- Blackstone owned for profit provider signs management agreement with large housing association (*Inside Housing*, 13 March 2019)
- Billionaire property family invests in social housing company (*Inside Housing*, 24 January 2019)
- BNP Paribas issues £100 million credit facility to L&Q Housing Association (*Social Housing* [online], 26 June 2018)
- Cross Keys Homes takes £80 million loan from Swedish bank (*Inside Housing*, 24 November 2017)

Another deal that hit the headlines early in 2019 was the announcement from CBRE of a Global Investors Fund that was making £250 million available from a consortium of private funders and institutions to invest in a UK affordable housing fund.[3] The small print told a slightly different story. The fund is not primarily for affordable housing, but for shared ownership and housing for key workers, both of which can be highly profitable. In other words, the Global Investors Fund is aiming at professionals who are unable to buy at current prices and forced to rent in the private market. The 'affordable housing' label is very useful to attract public sector partners, but who would bet on the number of social housing units that are likely to be actually built? The financial risks and the lack of public accountability are obvious. The banking sector believes that their loans are safe because housing associations are partly in the public sector and will be bailed out by the government. However, the associations are taking big risks with their tenants.

One such case is the First Priority Housing Association, a supported housing provider with a head office in New Malden, Essex, which plunged close to insolvency in 2018 over leasing deals with private equity and hedge fund investors. First Priority does not own or build its own properties, but leases them from investor groups. An *Inside Housing* investigation found that First Priority had 759 tenancies in 277 properties owned by 27 different investors. When a number of properties became empty, First Priority could not meet the terms of their leasing contracts, owing £2.9 million to creditors (Barratt, 2018b). Days after this story was published, it emerged that First Priority was the tip of the iceberg, with at least two other housing associations identified as financed through risky private equity schemes. There are now multiple reports of housing associations leasing homes from investment funds facing the risk of being forced as landlords to cut back on services to tenants or increase rents to unacceptable levels in order to meet the demands of investors (Riddy, 2018).

Speculation with public assets and social tenancies is part of a wider picture in which local authorities are also entering into risky loan agreements with private banks and hedge funds instead of obtaining loans from the conventional source, the Public Works Loan Board (PWLB). The PWLB is a government funding body that issues loans from the National Loans Fund at Treasury-determined interest rates. Some local authorities are being tricked into buying 'teaser rate' loans based on derivatives offered by brokers, bankers and financial advisers. A public campaign is being mounted against these so called 'LOBO' (Lender Option; Borrowing Option) loans, not least because they are highly confidential and undermine local democracy, quite apart from putting local services at risk.[4]

It can be argued that local authorities are being forced into these measures by government-imposed limits on local authority borrowing. However, some authorities are going well beyond their remit into risky property ventures that are not fully transparent, putting their tenants and residents at risk. In the process, these partnerships and financial deals between councils, housing associations and City finance have turned the politics of housing upside down. To its obvious delight, the property lobby has found new and previously unexpected allies in housing associations and local councils, who are signing up as members and affiliates to the HBF and the BPF.

A world away

All this is a world away from the municipal origins of local councils. In the 1930s and the post-war period, there was an honourable tradition of municipal socialism in parts of the UK. Many local councils provided as much of a local welfare state for their residents as they were able to, with housing and social services built and managed by the local authority in a tradition of altruism and social responsibility. Council housing was built on council-owned land, not for profit, but to meet need. Rents were set on the basis of what people could afford – and tenancies were for life (Bowie, 2017). Now, we have the opposite: as central government has cut back grants and powers to local councils, local councils have been scrambling to sell off assets and to invest in commercial property ventures. Council houses and land have become financial assets to be traded for capital gain and income return. Council rents and tenancy contracts are set on an increasingly commercial basis corresponding closely with rents and tenancies in the private sector.

As each economic crisis has hit and public finances have been reined in, a further screw has been put on social and affordable housing, and councils have increased their search for profits from their own land and property. As we have already seen, the 2008 financial crash intensified the ideological debate about public services. This includes 'sweating assets' to fund services. Local councils have been under pressure externally, as well as internally from their own accountants and advisers, to raise rents, sell land and enter into commercial partnerships with the development sector. This is what financialisation means in practice (Albeers, 2016).

A similar journey has been taken as we have seen by housing associations. Once a social movement of the 1970s built on the charitable housing movement of the Victorian era (with the likes of Peabody and Octavia Hill), housing associations are now entangled with financial investors and property dealers. The Housing Act 1988 started the rot, encouraging the contentious transfer of housing stock from local authority ownership to housing associations. The real financial entanglement began in the 1990s as direct funding from the government was steadily reduced and associations were encouraged to seek funding from the private sector. Government funding stopped completely in the early years of the Coalition government, and social housing provision by housing associations became entirely dependent on City funding. In the past, housing association staff were primarily concerned with the welfare of their tenants; now, they are focused on profit margins and the financial viability of their business models. While it was commonplace in the 2000s to include an element of commercial development in their schemes in order to cross-subsidise social and affordable housing, they have now moved on to straight commercial borrowing and building for sale. Many have now dropped their charitable status on government advice to become Registered Social Landlords (RSLs) with more ability to access government and private funding support. The result is that some large housing associations are becoming property businesses and public limited companies (PLCs), rather than the principled not-for-profit social housing organisations that they grew out of.

Light at the end of the tunnel or more spin?

Some in the social housing movement are hopeful that this cannot go on. After the 2017 election that produced a minority government, Whitehall began to be more flexible. There were suggestions of more support for social housing: dropping the demonisation of social housing tenants, especially after the Grenfell fire disaster; offering more funding to housing associations; and, at last, encouraging councils to start building council housing again. In 2018, the government promised to lift the borrowing cap that prevented councils from borrowing money to build council housing. A new Minister for Housing stated: 'Councils in England have an important role to play to make sure enough new homes are built in the right places and need to be in the frontline of new home construction' (Clancy, 2018). This is a typically ambiguous statement from ministers; good news if it means more money for social housing or bad if councils are being told to grant more permissions to the volume housebuilders. On the plus side, the government has also begun in a small way to fund community land trusts and custom build schemes through a special three-year Community Housing Fund, which, at £60 million a year, is tiny but a move in the right direction.

As we noted earlier, in 2018, the government announced that it was to allocate £2 billion over ten years to housing associations and was to lift the borrowing cap for local authorities. The £2 billion might sound a lot but it translates into just £200 million per year across the whole of England. At the average cost of land and construction for a new house of say £200,000, this amounts to 1,000 affordable homes per annum. Compare this to the annual output of Barratt of 17,000 new homes a year. Housing experts say that the pot will need to be tripled to £6 billion a year if we are reach the 90,000 extra social homes needed per annum to deal with the housing crisis. This is not impossible. The National Housing Federation notes that in 1975/76 investment in social housing was £18 billion a year but in 2014/15 it was just £1.2 billion (National Housing Federation, 2018).

Deep frustration at the lack of government action on building council or other forms of social housing, and anger over the continuation of the Right to Buy policy, have led many councils to take unilateral action of their own. Research commissioned by the RTPI showed that both Conservative and Labour councils have found ways to start building council houses again at a small scale, often through setting up their own housing companies (Morphet, 2017). A least 50 local authorities have set up their own housing companies that aim to build on their own land, and as private companies, they escape the Right to Buy legislation.

Does this mean that financialisation of housing is over? I am afraid that it does not. First, as long as the Right to Buy remains on the statute books, depleting social housing stock, including new homes, it undermines any new building by councils or housing associations. Second, and more significant in the long term, councils and housing associations are sceptical that the government will put direct funding into council housebuilding and will therefore force local authorities to continue to borrow from the markets to raise capital for affordable housing, and to continue with cross-subsidy. The overarching narrative that government will not fund social housing at the required level and that private finance should play a bigger role in social and affordable housing provision remains firmly in place. With this support behind it, the finance sector is obliging. Third, many councils, particularly in London and the South East, have already sold off their precious land

and housing assets. They have missed the boat for building on their own land, and must start buying land all over again – at exorbitant prices.

Finally, financialisation is not just about business plans; it is a managerial culture drawing in all of the built environment professions, including the planners, housing officers and senior councillors in local and central government. Council and housing association officers have moved in and out of property consultancies in a revolving door that we noted earlier. Financialisation has become addictive for many chief executives and council leaders – they have made their careers on it – and they may not wish to shift away from their 'business-first' approach to look again at core public service values. Therefore, financialisation is not going away anytime soon.

Conclusion

The financialisation trap has created a rift in the social and affordable housing movement. While many of the large associations and councils are embracing private finance, smaller housing charities and community land trusts take a more wary view. Going into the marketplace to borrow money may be necessary in the absence of government funding, but there are grave dangers of embracing private finance to get into the government's good books and potentially losing the connection with the core purpose and values of the social housing sector, particularly if the rents set by not-for-profit housing groups are unaffordable to those in housing need. Ultimately, the embrace of private finance will increase the lack of trust between those in housing need and the social and affordable sectors.

Dealing with the private sector comes with strings attached, and at the moment, these are almost entirely negative to the core purpose of the social and affordable housing sector. Private finance conditions about tenure, rent levels and commercial returns are damaging and counterproductive, and so is the default lack of public scrutiny over public–private partnership deals. A political divide is emerging between those who want a decisive break with financialisation and a return to council and not-for-profit housing, and those who still believe they can make the public–private partnership model work.

In Chapter 10, we look at examples of how financialisation has been introduced into planning and housing policy at the local level. Two case studies – one in Oxford, the other in Barking Reach in London – demonstrate how local authority dependence on private finance and landownership works in practice, and the implications for providing the housing that communities need.

10

Local case studies

The stranglehold of the finance–housebuilder complex over housing and planning is not just taking place remotely at a national level; it directly intrudes into local planning decision-making in your city, town and neighbourhood. Almost every major local planning decision about housing and development is influenced by the bigger picture of the business model of the housebuilders and landowners, and by government (and local government) dependency on it.

Oxford North

This first case study focuses on a single planning application in the city of Oxford, a local authority in the South East of England under intense pressure to provide more affordable housing. It traces how the pressures of the finance–housebuilding complex come together to influence day-to-day plan making and development control decisions at a local level. The Oxford North scheme is a large mixed-use development not unlike many housing developments promoted by local authorities and landowners across the country.

Oxford has been described as the least affordable place in the UK. In 2018, average house prices, at £435,000, were 17.5 times the average incomes of Oxford residents. There are 3,300 households on the housing waiting list and 100 households each month presenting to the council as homeless and requiring assistance. The city estimates that it needs 24,000–32,000 additional homes between 2011 and 2031 but there is space for only 7,500 within the city boundaries. In other words, it is a city bursting at the seams and desperately short of social and affordable housing.[1]

With the city constrained by its boundaries and surrounding green belt, and with a booming economy, land and property are at a premium. It should be a circumstance where the local authority has extraordinary leverage over developers and landowners in the content, design and affordable housing planning obligations of development schemes. There is surely enough rising land value to require a high level of affordable housing obligations to be met without harming landowner or developer profits.

However, this is far from the full story. Housing development in Oxford is controlled largely by university landowners and student housing landlords. The largest landowners (and the wealthiest) in the city are the Oxford colleges and Oxford University itself. A survey published in May 2018 revealed that 36 Oxford colleges have a combined wealth of £5.8 billion and Oxford University has £3.2 billion. St John's, the richest college, has wealth of £592 million (Greenwood and Adams, 2018). Much of this wealth is tied up in land across the city centre, in the outer suburbs and villages, and far and wide across South East England. Yet, this wealth is not available to the community. Its historic landownership and thousand-year association with the city of Oxford and its communities are irrelevant to how it conducts its property transactions.

It is perhaps not well known that the Oxford colleges, like many universities, are charitable educational institutions that do not pay tax on profits from trading or from the sale of property assets. They also pay only 20 per cent of business rates on non-domestic property. Local residents in the shadow of the ultra-wealthy Oxford colleges pay more for council services than their wealthy educational business neighbours. It turns out that the colleges also routinely seek to reduce their planning obligations because they say that their student housing schemes should not be liable for Section 106 because they are not normal residential dwellings. Yet, in every respect, the colleges are businesses seeking to make a profit. Thus, St John's College has its own financial and property advisers, and expects to make a commercial return like any other landowner or developer.

Oxford North is a large site within the boundaries of the city of Oxford, which is very well located and capable of large-scale development. It comprises 26 hectares alongside the Oxford ring road on the northern edge of the city. The site is bisected by three major roads – the A40, the A34 and the A44 and is only half a mile from a mainline railway station to London – and has relatively little existing development on site. The land is described in the application as 'open fields', that is, agricultural grazing land. An Area Action Plan (AAP) produced by the council in 2015 proposed a mixed development of industry and housing, comprising 90,000 square metres for 4,500 jobs and 500 homes. Of the 500 homes, following council policy, 50 per cent would be affordable homes, and of these, 80 per cent would be social homes; thus, there would be 200 social rented homes and 50 affordable homes, a potentially important contribution to helping out with Oxford's housing crisis.

Thomas White Oxford (TWO), a commercial development consultancy wholly owned by St John's College, produced a glossy brochure for Oxford North. The vision is described as creating 'Oxford's New Urban District – a thriving and vibrant business community with innovation and sustainability at its heart'. The scheme will 'unlock previously inaccessible land to residents, visitors, and people passing through, transforming the area with tree lined streets and a mix of workplaces, homes, leisure and arts and culture'.[2] It promises £100 million of infrastructure investment and a sustainable community.

The main challenge to the scheme is the existing high level of traffic congestion at a strategic intersection of the A40 ring road, and the likelihood that Oxford North would make congestion much worse. Thus, major transport improvements were needed to 'unlock the site'. A significant package of public funding was assembled, totalling £10 million for transport improvements, plus £10 million from Homes England for affordable housing and a further £5.9 million from the Local Growth Fund.

A planning application was submitted in July 2018 by TWO. The £500 million scheme followed the council's AAP in all respects but one: there would be zero affordable housing. A viability assessment by TWO consultants Savills claimed that the scheme would be unviable if the required amount of affordable housing was provided. This was in spite of the 90,000 square metres of commercial floor space and the offer of substantial grant funding.

The college has no historic costs and only negligible ongoing costs associated with its ownership. If they get a planning consent, there will be at least a hundredfold increase in the value of the land, some arising from the publicly funded road infrastructure, the rest from the development of housing and high-tech employment. There is more than enough uplift in value and developer profit to pay for all the affordable housing that the council needs – and more. Yet, the TWO starting position is zero affordable housing. How can this be?

TWO consultants Savills produced a viability assessment that shows a negative residual value from the development. The land value was put into the viability model at £12.4 million even though the site is in agricultural use and has been in St John's ownership for generations. Its value as agricultural land is very much lower, around £0.63 million. The long-term uplift of the value of the site due to the transport investment is ignored entirely in the viability assessment. The huge potential uplift in value that could pay for all the affordable housing required by the council was largely hidden in the viability assessment. The outcry that followed the planning application led TWO to undertake further analysis of the costs of the scheme, testing the impact of 25 per cent and 30 per cent affordable housing. It concluded that despite the initial viability assessment that only zero affordable housing was possible, 35 per cent affordable housing (and a review mechanism) was, in fact, possible. Although still far from the 50 per cent affordable housing policy of the council, this shift in position illustrates the cynicism of the viability assessment process

St John's College first demands a public subsidy to develop the site, most of it already in their ownership, and then refuses to build the affordable housing that the city needs in spite of the huge uplift in value from the planning consent and the immense wealth of the college. Although this development will create a significant demand for health services, no funding is to be provided for this. New residents and workers in Oxford North will have to travel into Oxford to get a place in already overcrowded surgeries. Two primary schools half a mile from the site will need to be expanded. Who is going to pay for that? The police asked for additional resources from the developers to deal with extra demands from 4,500 jobs and 500 new homes, but this was refused on the grounds that this would affect the viability of the scheme. Nor did the applicant say who the actual developer of the site would be. Who is going to get the profits from the high-tech industrial space and the housing? Much of this will presumably go to St John's. One would have thought these matters were material and that the local council would want answers to these questions.

Local people certainly want to know the full facts, and as is so common in viability cases, communities have zero trust in property consultants and have to undertake their own viability assessments. Thus in Oxford North, neighbourhood forums in the vicinity of the development and the Civic Society undertook their own viability assessment of the scheme and concluded that, contrary to TWO and St John's assertions, the actual level of profit from the scheme will allow the policy compliant level of affordable housing to be met.

What was also curious from the public point of view was that at no time in the AAP or in the report of the public inquiry into the AAP was there any specific mention of who the owners of the site were or their connection to Oxford; indeed, there was no section in the reports on who owned the land, or the implications of this landownership for the content of the development scheme, or its delivery. St John's College is never named despite the fact that it is the most prominent and wealthiest college in Oxford and has owned this land for generations. Bearing in mind its tax exemptions and also that its land is of agricultural value, one would have thought that at least some of the profits and the huge uplift in value would go back to the community – instead of into St John's. Consultants for the developers claimed that they had to follow RICS guidance which says a viability calculation has to assume 'a blind assessment', using the concept of a 'typical developer' and 'typical landowner' (RICS, 2017). In other words, the actual facts of the development were totally hidden from sight.

This saga perfectly illustrates the gaming of the planning system. The developer, TWO, claimed that they cannot afford any affordable housing because their viability assessment says so. Then, under pressure, the developer says that, as a favour, they will, in fact, provide more affordable housing. The viability assessment is thus not a fixed point, but a negotiating tactic – a cynical game to intimidate the council and the community, enabling landowners and developers to get away with less than the 50 per cent affordable housing set down in council policy.

This is not an unusual case. Part of the problem is that many local authorities are not equipped to interrogate viability assessments or lack the political will to uncover what is really going on. We have noted that planners rarely name the landowner or do due diligence on the developer. Airbrushing of the names of landowners is normal practice. Town planning officers and councillors follow to the letter the dictum that planning is about the 'use of land not its ownership'. The irony is that ownership and value are now, in fact, highly relevant since viability assessment was introduced into the NPPF. Privately planning officers know that they are being manipulated but they publicly keep quiet. Many local authorities are so desperate for new housing that they become the supplicants, and are afraid to go to appeal when applicants ignore their planning policies. Councils seem to abandon too readily their strongest negotiating cards: grant money and planning consents. In North Oxford, if the council had done its homework on the landowner's and developer's real costs and values, it could fully justify the 50 per cent affordable housing set down in its local plan policy, and show that there is more than enough value left for St John's.

Barking, East London

The London borough of Barking and Dagenham is an East London Thames-side borough with a mission to improve its housing stock. The housing waiting list numbers 7,000 households, and according to the council website, only 600 vacant homes become available each year. However, there is huge housing potential from vacant industrial land in the borough, much of it on the Thames-side. This case study concerns two development projects led by the council, Barking Town Centre and Barking Riverside. They each demonstrate the different ways in which a local authority has entered into partnerships with housebuilders and investment groups, and has become entangled with special development vehicles and finance groups such that local people are disempowered and shut out of key decisions.

In Barking Town Centre and Barking Riverside, the council owned land and buildings that it wanted to see redeveloped for housing. In 2011, it was approached by Laing O'Rourke, a building company, and an investment group called Long Harbour. Long Harbour was founded in 2009 by William Waldorf Astor IV of the aristocratic Astor family, who was also the half-brother of the soon-to-be Prime Minister David Cameron's wife Samantha. The company is a fund management company that makes profits from asset value accumulation. It offered to lend Barking and Dagenham Council £73 million to build 477 affordable homes: 200 in the Town Centre and 277 on the Riverside. The terms were an interest rate of 3.5 per cent adjusted for inflation to be paid over 60 years. The land would remain in Long Harbour ownership for 60 years and only after that would the council come into ownership of the site. The individual homes on the site could be sold but the terms required them to be replaced so that there were always 477 homes under contract. As a sweetener for Long Harbour, the Homes and Communities Agency gave the scheme a generous grant. The housebuilders would be Laing O'Rourke.

There was no public consultation on the deal or its implications for the council or its tenants. Yet, the financial deal was the driver behind the whole development, locking the council in for 60 years. It required rent increases to keep pace with repayments to Long Harbour. If rents did not keep pace because the rental market dipped, the council would have to find the money from elsewhere.

Unfortunately, shortly after the new homes came on stream, market rents in the Barking and Dagenham area did drop, immediately putting the council in difficulty. None of this bothered Long Harbour. They are an investment company, not community developers. They sold the deal on to other investors, first to a Hong Kong consortium, who, in turn, sold it on to HSBC, trapping the council even further in financial mire. The contract offered no get-out or break clause, or review clause. To pay off the debt, the council required the rent to go up on a regular basis, clearly against the interests of its own residents. This was pure financialisation of council assets, trapping the council in a web of City finance. The final indignity for those on the housing waiting list was that the scheme required the demolition of 277 council flats that were to be replaced with 232 affordable units, of which only 72 were for social rent.

Barking Riverside is often described as one of the largest development sites in Europe. It covers 175 hectares along the River Thames to the east of London Docklands in what was called the Thames Gateway. The borough is famous for housing the Ford Plant at Dagenham close to the Riverside area. Barking Riverside, with potential for 50,000 homes, presents a major opportunity to tackle the housing crisis in the borough.

Part of Barking Riverside was formerly the site of Barking Power Station and was owned by National Power. It was sold to Bellway Homes, who obtained a grant to reclaim the land. Bellway then built 900 units for private sale, with the scheme attracting criticism for the lack of affordable housing, schools and community facilities. A *Guardian* article described the scheme as 'No cafe, no pub, no doctor, in London's most isolated suburb' (Burrows, 2015).

Subsequently, a master plan for 6,000 homes was produced by the council, this time seeking 25 per cent affordable housing and promising an extension of the Docklands Light Railway to Barking Riverside. Bellway Homes built a further 900 homes. A new master plan was produced in 2013 proposing a further 10,800 homes predicated on the extension of the Docklands Light Railway.

However, shortly after the master plan was published, the proposed extension of the Docklands Light Railway was cancelled. A replacement rail link was proposed, extending the Gospel Oak Overground line from Barking Town Centre to Barking Riverside to be partly paid for by the Barking Riverside Consortium (English Partnerships and Bellway Homes) and partly by Transport for London. Meanwhile, the share of Barking Riverside owned by Bellway Homes was bought out by London and Quadrant Housing, enabling Bellway to move out after having made huge profits subsidised by Homes England, and having borne very little of the liabilities (or transport infrastructure costs) for Barking Riverside.

A new company was formed, Barking Riverside Limited, comprising London and Quadrant and the GLA, who now owned much of the land. The council's corporate plan describes the new scheme for the Riverside as 'Barcelona on Thames'. It envisages private investment of £60 million. Barking and Dagenham Council says that its aim is 'inclusive growth', that is, it aims to include the community and its needs at every stage. This good intention did not begin well. A community interest company set up by the council to provide community input initially placed no local residents on the company board. As I write, the participation of local residents on the community interest company board is unresolved. It is an all too common example of the determination of authorities to limit community involvement in public-private partnership schemes even when the banner headline is 'inclusive growth'.

In the midst of the debate about the local governance of Barcelona on Thames, a fire broke out in a block of Bellway-built flats in Barking Reach in June 2019. Twenty flats were gutted but, fortunately, all residents were evacuated safely. However, residents said that there were no alarms or sprinklers in the flats even though the flats were clad in wood. Just as at Grenfell, neither the council nor the developers were willing to take responsibility for causing the fire or for paying compensation (Apps, 2019).

The Barking flats fire illustrates exactly the lack of accountability that is now deeply embedded in urban development in the UK because of the complex deals that local authorities have entered into in their search for land and funding for housing. In these deals, the numbers of units come first but the provision of community infrastructure and the needs of tenants and residents seem to come last.

Conclusion

The case studies are not a scientific sample, but are drawn from the author's own experience. There are countless other examples in local newspapers, in planning journals and on community websites, but the two I have chosen illustrate a number of truths about the planning and housing system that cannot be avoided any longer:

- Contrary to developer/landowner arguments that their investments are high risk, in fact, local authorities and the government take much of the risks from development. They fund essential infrastructure, give grants for affordable housing and take the political risk of bending their local plan policies to meet developer viability arguments. Despite the careful wording of local plans that communities have fought over at local plan inquiries, it turns out that there is no certainty about them. They are aspirations not policies, and far too often, they are simply negotiated away with the community standing by helpless.
- The land value created by publicly funded infrastructure and the grant of planning permission is siphoned off by the landowner and developer – local authorities and communities get back only a fraction in planning gain.

- The amount, price, quality and timing of affordable housing are dependent not on local plan policy, but on negotiations over the profitability of development in which the development sector has far more power. So-called 'planning obligations', it turns out, are not obligations at all.
- Planners in town halls do not routinely investigate the crucial property market factors underlying development schemes such as the implications of landownership, financing and due diligence for the deliverability, quality and sustainability of development schemes. In other words, they are not in control and cannot realistically deliver the 'sustainable development' outcomes that the NPPF requires.
- Planners are woefully under-resourced and have outsourced much of what they do to consultants, leading to a loss of public accountability and the creation of unacceptable conflicts of interest.
- The financialisation of housing and development has encouraged development deals that are cloaked in 'commercial confidentiality' clauses and opt-outs, in which local authorities and housing associations very often collude. Partnership deals and ownership are traded on the financial markets (or behind closed doors in councils) so that there is often no connection between those who own and undertake new housing development and the communities who live there. There is an alarming lack of public accountability and inadequate public scrutiny. None of this is inevitable or necessary. It is a choice made by local and central governments.
- Finally, these truths are not confined to one political party or one city; they are endemic. They are system-wide, and have become institutional. To be sure, there is variation from place to place and some local negotiations are very much better than others, but the asymmetry of power between local authorities/communities and the property sector has ensured that the housing and planning crisis goes on and on without respite.

These problems with local planning control are a reflection of the largely hidden finance–housebuilder complex that now entraps the UK housing and planning system. In Chapter 11, we turn to the ideas, policies and proposals that could begin to tackle these deep-seated practices and blockages to change.

11

Unblocking the impasse

Tackling the housing crisis has reached an impasse. Despite countless reports and government announcements over decades, nothing in housing seems to change for the better – not enough new homes are built, prices keep going up, affordability gets worse, the young are priced out and homeless numbers grow. Local communities are deeply dissatisfied with the planning and housing system. Local authorities are continually on the defensive from development pressure and are having rings run round them by developers, landowners and property consultants. Meanwhile, we await the almost inevitable property slump after the boom years of the mid-2010s.

This book seeks to answer the question of why nothing seems to change – and what we should do about it. It is unacceptable that property market forces seem so powerful and the government so complicit that the housing crisis has become a fixed part of life in the 21st-century UK. It is imperative to find out why we are so trapped and then to do something about it. The argument of this book is that there is no mystery to the current crisis. There is an alignment of the finance–housebuilding complex and the government perpetuating, and, at times, manufacturing, the housing crisis to suit their interests. The property lobby is so powerful and pervasive that no government and no local authority seem able to resist it. Indeed, as this book shows, there is a virtual conspiracy by market players to deliberately limit the amount of housing to keep land and house prices on an ever-rising trajectory, with governments unwilling to challenge it because they rely on a rising property market for taxation and political donations. This is the hidden reality of power behind the housing crisis that must be tackled if we, the people, are to unblock the impasse.

In the Preface to the book, Ted's story tells of a community in South London literally priced out by commercial development pressure, with seemingly nothing that local authorities are able to do about it. In fact, what is worse, local councils seem wittingly or unwittingly to collude with developers and landowners in the loss of social and affordable housing, and the social and cultural life that goes with it. Ted's community, like many others, has been overrun by by luxury flats, offices and high-end restaurants. Nor is this loss of community, social housing and sense of place only a city phenomenon.

The Preface gave an example of how another branch of the property market, the volume housebuilders, has a stranglehold on housebuilding far from London in Northamptonshire. What these two areas – North Southwark and Northamptonshire – and many others, have in common is that the town planners, communities and local authorities in both areas are no match for the developers, housebuilders and landowners in negotiations over housing numbers, the mix of tenure, the amount of affordable housing, design standards or the provision of essential community facilities such as health centres, shops and new schools. An entirely new approach is needed.

The housing shortage is no accident

The housing shortage is not an accident. Shortages keep prices up. Price rises have become a strategic underpinning of the UK economy, its mortgage market and its investment markets. Where price growth is everything, shortages are essential. It is no surprise, although it is of course denied, that housebuilders and landowners rely upon shortages and price rises to underpin their business model. They will not build out their vast land banks quickly to meet demand because it will reduce ticket prices on their new homes.

The housebuilding market is not a free market. Nor is the land market that underlies it. 'The market for development land in the UK is rigged' – this is the conclusion of Cahill (2001:14), who examined landownership in the UK and documented the small number of large landowners who dominate the market. He estimates that 157,000 individuals and families control 26 million acres of the UK, and that as recently as 2001, nearly a third of land in the British Isles is in the hands of aristocrats and the landed gentry. The top ten private landowners own 2.5 million acres (Cahill, 2001). Shrubsole (2019) has calculated that 1 per cent of the population own half of England. It goes without saying that this select group of owners has immense power over development and the housing crisis.

Of course, it is denied, but there are strong indications that landowners and developers in housing growth areas work together to ensure that land and new housing are released and 'drip-fed' onto the market to keep up prices. It makes economic sense for them to manage the market together in this way so that no one operator takes unfair advantage of another by releasing sites, or building out too quickly, or reducing prices below agreed norms. They benefit, but not the hundreds of thousands that desperately need housing that is affordable. We have shown how repeated government-inspired reviews of the housebuilding sector over the past ten years have cleared developers and landowners of land hoarding and price fixing. The reviews have been undertaken by government-appointed property market insiders and Conservative MPs – so it is not surprising that they would clear the property sector of fixing the market.

The inevitable conclusion is that the property sector in all its forms is a major blocker for change in how housing is supplied in this country. Their business model, now almost completely integrated with property investors and financial institutions, dominates the delivery, price, location and design of new housing. It is a model that is fiercely defended by the property professions, notably, the influential RICS, and by government planning inspectors and valuation panels. The government fully accepts this business model with little challenge or criticism because it relies upon the volume housebuilders to deliver its housing targets, and much more. The government poured billions into the property market to bail it out after the financial crash through direct grants and QE, and continues long after the financial crash to pump money directly into the volume housebuilding sector and landowners through Help to Buy, tax breaks, subsidies and infrastructure loans.

The power of the property lobby

The property lobby has unparalleled political connections, including direct access to government ministers and senior representatives of political parties; as we have seen, it boasts of its success in influencing national and local policies on housing and town planning to their own advantage. The lobby is not always united – landowners, developers, financiers and landlords sometimes represent different interests. However, they have consistently come together to defend their red lines – light planning regulation, government financial support and limited intervention in the land market – and consequently high prices and housing shortages. The property professions, such as the RICS, have legitimised these red lines by codifying professional practices which ensure that property professionals benefit from the fees that can be obtained from the current system. At the same time, they create a professional aura that gives them the ear of ministers, top civil servants and the Treasury, who, in turn, rely upon the RICS for advice on property policy.

By comparison, local authorities, at the front line of the housing crisis, who actually understand what housing stress means to people, have lost much of their lobbying power as their economic and democratic role has been cut back by successive governments. Of course, governments listen to them politely, but it does not give nearly as much weight to their views as it does to the finance–housebuilding complex. Partly, this is because of the power wielded by City finance, but there is a cruder political reason: advocating funding for social and affordable housing has a lower political priority to governments of all colours than support for homeownership. The not-for-profit housing sector tries hard to get the ear of the media and politicians, and has strong support among specialised housing professionals and among voluntary and community organisations. However, as a provider of housing, it is seen as lightweight and costly by the government, as compared with the big housebuilders, banks and financial institutions (whose own subsidies are always ignored when it comes to talking about the 'burdens of public expenditure'). Moreover, it is plain to see that property companies support the Conservative Party ideologically and financially while the social housing sector is seen as lobbying for other parties. In this lobbying contest, you can imagine where the sympathy of HM Treasury lies.

The crucial point about this imbalance of power is that it reflects quite accurately how the vast quantum of land value created by development across the country is distributed between rich and poor, that is, who gets the benefit. We rely upon taxation to redistribute most of this windfall but the tax mechanism has failed. Successive governments have not taxed development gain anywhere near enough and the property sector has become masterful at hiding the values it creates from the HMRC. Capital gains tax exists at the national level but avoiding or reducing it is routine, for example, by creating trusts and registering offshore. Planning obligations (Section 106 and CIL) are the only mechanisms available at a local level but they are now being avoided by viability assessment. The result is that the largest slice of land value uplift by far is taken directly by landowners, banks and developers, leaving only a small fraction for local authorities or communities. Each extra slice held back by market players in negotiation with local authorities reduces the amount available for social and affordable housing, public services, good design and genuine sustainable development.

It must be stressed that government commitment to 'sustainable development' in the planning system does not correct this imbalance. The property lobby and the Treasury have ensured that the NPPF says that a precondition for sustainable development is that development must be financially viable or 'deliverable'. In effect, instead of the concept of sustainability being a policy to rebalance the economic distribution of land value and embrace environmental stewardship, the planning system makes sustainability subordinate to viability, deliverability and growth.

The gigantic loss of land value to localities, and the disempowerment of local government, over the past 40 years mean that local authorities have been stripped of their capacity to plan positively for their communities. They are unable to plan, build or buy anywhere near the amount of social housing required to reduce waiting lists or to undertake proper master planning or 'place making'. Master planning has been replaced by negotiation over viability, as the Old Oak Common example in Chapter 8 showed. That is the new version of 'bottom-up' planning, in other words, not planning from the needs of communities upwards, but from the demands of the landowners and financiers upwards. In an attempt to compensate, some local authorities have fallen into the trap of becoming commercial developers themselves, trying to extract some small quantity of 'affordable' housing from complex development deals. It is a sorry sight when local authorities are drumming up business by attending international property fairs like the infamous MIPIM fair held annually in Cannes, or becoming signed-up members of commercial property lobby groups. Many local communities are finding it difficult to tell the difference between some local authority and housing association developers and the commercial developers themselves.

The catch-22 of the housing crisis, which is a gift for the property industry, is that existing homeowners want the value of their homes to go up. The media presents house prices going down or even standing still as a near disaster – and it is true that most homeowners would be unhappy if developers started selling homes round the corner from their own home at significantly less than their own home was worth. However, addiction to rising house prices has a big downside, as succinctly put in an article in *The Guardian* (2018): 'Britain's passion for rising house prices is both strange and irrational because by any yardstick a surging property market is bad news. It makes people wealthier than they actually are so encourages them to take on more debt than they can afford.'

The politics of the housing crisis

How under these circumstances can a coalition of interests be mobilised to do something serious about affordability and the housing crisis? At the very least, if land and house prices were more stable, as they are in many North-West European countries with less property-dependent economies, and if those in housing need were provided with genuinely affordable homes, the system would be less divisive between renters and homeowners, and between public versus private housing. Moreover, perhaps market stability would switch a fraction of the vast quantity of speculative property investment into more productive parts of the economy and society. To bring about this stability will require a significant change in how we think about housing in the UK.

As a nation, we must stop relying upon the finance–housebuilding complex to build the housing that the country needs. This complex cannot and will not do this; it is not their job. They exist to make profits for their shareholders, not to deliver national housing policy. The public have been misled because the government has told people that by supporting the profitability of the sector, communities can benefit from cross-subsidy, in other words, building genuinely affordable housing from a proportion of the profits of the housebuilders. It is also widely believed that increased housing output will, on its own, bring prices down. As discussed earlier, it will not. The problem is that the profitability of the housebuilding sector is in contradiction with the housing that the country needs. As for cross-subsidy, time and again it has failed to deliver sufficient social and affordable housing.

The housing crisis is also a planning crisis

The housing crisis is intimately tied up with the planning system. The town planning system has been expertly gamed by the housebuilders to their benefit. Reform of the planning system will not solve the housing crisis, but without radical reform of planning, the housing crisis will never be resolved. We urgently need a planning system that cannot be gamed. However, more than that, we also need a planning system that does a lot more than allowing the construction of housing: it must provide genuinely sustainable development with a full range of public services. The current property-led planning system is not fit for this purpose (Ellis and Henderson, 2016).

The housebuilder lobby has mounted a sustained attack on planning for decades. Yet, despite these claims, the town planning system has little to do with causing the housing crisis. Town planning can allocate land for housing and it can implore that affordable housing is built, but it cannot require that land is developed, or that certain levels of rent or tenure must be provided. It can try to ensure high specifications and decent standards of housing and amenities, and that is very important, but, as we have seen, these standards are often negotiated away or ignored – and developers get away with it. Planning itself cannot deliver the quality, affordability or sustainability of housing development under the current system. Only if planning is allied to the means to design, build, develop and set rent levels can it deliver.

It is a little-known fact that planning law does not allow planning authorities to distinguish land use by tenure. There is no separate use class for 'social housing' or 'affordable housing', only for 'a dwelling house' or 'a house in multiple occupation'. Thus, in law, a local planning authority cannot refuse a planning application for luxury flats because they are unaffordable, or because they are homes for sale on a particular site rather than social rented homes. Despite all the government rhetoric about 'delivery', the planning system is not empowered to deliver new homes. It can grant or refuse planning permission but cannot refuse an application because it is from a speculative developer, or because the applicant is simply trying to increase the value of the site and sell it on. It cannot compel a developer to build. In law, planning decisions must be about 'land use', not value; yet, perversely, the property development system is almost entirely about value. Thus, there are real limits to how much town planning can regulate tenure, price, affordability or the nature of the occupant or owner. Only in exceptional circumstances can planning law consider 'human factors' such as the circumstances of the owner or occupier (Moore, 1987).

This is not to argue that reforms of the planning system are not needed; they are. The recent reviews and recommendations for reform from the RTPI and the TCPA (the Raynsford Review: TCPA, 2018b) that urge a reinvention of planning as a positive force in society are essential, but they will not produce more social and affordable housing on their own. This concern is not new. Ball's (1983: 245) study of housebuilders and planning in 1983 concluded that 'planning is in profound crisis'. Nearly 40 years later, the Raynsford Review describes the planning system as 'underfunded and demoralised', and 'significantly less powerful than at any time since 1947' (TCPA, 2018b: 50). It notes that the planning system has been twisted to the single aim of enabling private sector housing delivery, to the detriment of other objectives, and calls for a new consensus. However, a new consensus over planning is not likely to be achieved with the current adversarial position taken by the land and property market. Only if this market is reformed and properly regulated will the planning reforms correctly urged by the TCPA and many others, such as the Highbury Housing Group.[1]

'Good' developers will not help either

Some reformer politicians, afraid of challenging the market, cling to the idea that there are 'good' developers out there that are not so greedy and would be willing partners in ensuring balanced housing development. They hope that if there were more 'good' developers, the conflicts between developers and local authorities would be reduced. In reality, these developers/landowners are small in number. Furthermore, when looked at in detail, they depart only slightly from the mainstream business model of land banking, and, in practice, rarely stand up to be counted against the clamour of the property lobby. The views of the HBF, the CLA and the LPDF on land value capture, planning obligations and CPOs are not going to change because of a few good developers.

A national housing drive

As a nation, we must create a parallel housing development system to deliver for those in need of social and affordable housing, as well as the wide range of special needs housing – a system that must be separate from the volume housebuilders' property market. This was the case in the post-war period when housebuilding was seen as a national priority. When the private building sector was on its knees, the government had to step in. We need that sense of mission again – a national housing drive. Building social and affordable housing should be the role of the government – not on its own, but in partnership with local authorities, housing associations, communities and not-for-profit housing groups, each being encouraged (and part funded) to play a major role. The government and local authorities must be prepared to buy land and build themselves; however, equally importantly, they should legislate to allow a variety of not-for-profit local and national bodies to obtain development land at existing use value and access finance.

This mission should be part of a newly reinvigorated welfare state, where housing, like health, is available to those in need as a human right. The right to housing is not a new idea. It is enshrined in the Universal Declaration of Human Rights and the European Social Charter, and has been actively promoted in a number of countries. Yet, this means nothing without government action.

The starting principle is that good homes for everyone should be part of a healthy society. The health factor in housing is of immense importance because housing is a primary determinant of mental and physical health. In the post-war period, housing and health were part of the same government ministry. Civic society can clamour for a new national mission for social housing, as it has done, but the government must take the first step to make this happen.

The imperative of land reform

At the root of these proposals is land reform. Inequality in landownership is a major blocker to a national housing drive and achieving a decent level of housing affordability. Fear of land reform in England has for decades been a bogeyman created by newspapers and politicians, who talk wildly of the state taking over houses and gardens. This is, of course, nonsense. Public acquisition of ordinary houses with gardens is *not* part of land reform; the idea that land reform is about 'a garden tax' is just mischief making. The purpose of land reform is to bring development land forward for housing at sensible prices so that new housing can be truly affordable, and so that existing prices can stabilise. Andy Wightman (1996) has written and campaigned about the history of land reform in Scotland, where the inequality in landownership has been a more salient political issue than in England. As a result, significant steps have been taken to protect the crofting system, and in recent years, several underused landed estates in Scotland have been transferred to community ownership through land reform, notably, the Community Right to Buy legislation passed in 2003. A total of 500,000 acres of rural land in Scotland are now under community ownership (Field, 2020).

Wightman (1996: 190) makes the important point that the UK is exceptional in not having any regulations about who can buy land or how much they can own. Many countries prohibit the overseas purchase of certain categories of land and require agricultural land to be used productively for farming, not just held as an investment. Moreover, to dispel notions of a mass state takeover of private land, Wightman (1996: 193) argues that land reform should primarily be about an extension of community ownership facilitated by the state and an enhanced role for public ownership – and this is what is beginning to happen in Scotland. Yet, even in Scotland, the landownership registry is out of date, covering only 33 per cent of the land area. Wightman, now a member of the Scottish Parliament, assesses the current situation as 'a centuries long persistence of hegemonic landed power', concluding that 'Land reform has tinkered at the margins for too long' (Wightman, 1996).

England is in a much more backward state in terms of land policy than Scotland. Nothing approaching Scottish reforms has been attempted in England and Wales, where there is a similar gross inequality of landownership (Shrubsole, 2019). Outside Scotland, the national debate on landownership has effectively been shut down by the CLA and their long-term allies in the government, the Conservative Party. Cahill argues that the extreme disparity of landownership in Britain literally strangles the economy. Moreover, where land is publicly owned, it is being recklessly sold off by government instruction. In his study of public land in the UK, Brett Christophers (2018) reveals how public land has been sold off without any evidence that privatised land is now being used more efficiently, as claimed by its proponents. Yet, with growing public concern for inequality, and the clear-cut relationship of land to private wealth, now is the time to put land reform on the English political agenda.

In this book, we have noted that there has been a steady transformation of the traditional landowner sector into a commercial force. As Cahill discovered, the big landowners, with their aristocratic connections, have traditionally been given places on the boards of City institutions, banks and finance houses going back decades. Now, as landowner businesses, they are active in the financial markets, trading their land as investments. The new hegemony of landed power in the UK is shifting to the City of London, and is not confined to baronial estates in the countryside.

How do we tackle this formidable power structure? It must begin with transparency and the fair taxation of assets and landed wealth, as argued by Cahill, Wightman and Shrubsole, as well as by the Labour Party (2019) in *Land for the many*. So much land is not registered or is hidden from public scrutiny that billions of tax is lost to the Treasury each year. The Land Registry does not even record much of this land. The challenge of taxing land wealth and land sales fairly is an essential challenge for a just society. Capital gains tax for commercial land sales and transactions, particularly for companies and trusts, needs a complete overhaul to close its many loopholes and exemptions.

However, land reform is required for much more than that. It has a direct bearing on resolving the housing crisis. Land reform can bring about a wholly new approach to providing land for social and affordable housing, and for the capture of land value for the community. As we have seen, every plan to tackle these issues has failed over the past 60 years. The only local land value capture policies presently in use are Section 106, CIL and CPOs. Section 106 and CIL methods are deeply flawed by requirements about viability (as we examined in Chapter 6), and yet even in this watered-down form, they are under attack from the property lobby. The problem is not that these measures capture too much, as the landowners argue, but that they capture far too little, and are highly inefficient and expensive to operate.

As for CPOs used by local authorities to provide essential infrastructure or local development, they have become financially prohibitive because of the land compensation rules introduced in 1961 at the behest of the landowners' lobby, as we noted in Chapter 3. The Land Compensation Act 1961 (Section 5) is a major obstacle to the public development of land and should be repealed (Bentley, 2017). As the TCPA and a select committee of the House of Commons have noted, CPOs are urgently in need of updating and making a lot easier to use (MHCLG, 2018). Yet, this will not be easy because there is fierce resistance to repealing the 1961 Act from the CLA. The reform of CPO legislation will be a test case of whether the public or the landowners control land and planning in England.

Radical changes in public land acquisition and land value capture are a prerequisite if a future government is to seriously provide the big increase in social and affordable housing that Shelter and Crisis say the country needs. For this to be a reality, land acquisition by local authorities or community land trusts must be faster and cheaper. Specifically, land for genuinely affordable housing must be bought through an updated CPO process by public authorities at existing use value, excluding all hope value. There is nothing to be afraid of here. There are examples elsewhere that we can follow. In the Netherlands, local authorities buy up development land and undertake the servicing of sites, which are then offered to housebuilders, who build to the plans of the local authority (Falk, 2019). In this way, the housebuilders are simply builders of houses, not land speculators. Similar approaches are taken in Germany, where local authorities specify the housing mix, tenure and even price ranges of market homes.

Public legitimacy for the public and community acquisition of housing development land should be derived from local plans and neighbourhood plans adopted by local authorities and communities. The *Land for the many* report (2019) suggested the creation of a 'Common Ground Trust', which could buy land on behalf of homeowners who decided to become members of the trust so that they did not have to pay the extortionate cost of land when they bought a house. The planners have a key role to play in holding down the price of land by making clear in local plans that affordable and social housing policies must be adhered to whatever pressure is put on by landowners and developers. This will itself put a brake on land speculation.

It is important that land reforms are a collaboration with the community-led housing sector and the not-for-profit housing sector. For example, local authorities need to be willing to transfer serviced land at existing use value or on long leases to community land trusts or charitable housing bodies (Field, 2020). For some local authorities, this will require a cultural change: they will need to let go of the idea that their only credible partners are financiers and volume housebuilding companies.

Another approach to land reform that is more comprehensive and avoids the piecemeal capture of land value on a site-by-site basis is land value taxation. By taxing the increase in the value of land and property on a periodic basis, it is argued that there will be less incentive for landowners to hoard land and there will be more taxation income to redistribute for housing and other services. If a scheme covered all land, the stream of income will be sufficient to replace council tax and other property taxes.[2] Such a comprehensive approach to land would encourage more land to be brought forward for development. It is possible to imagine that, with the true decentralisation of powers from Whitehall – if ever that was to happen – individual towns and cities could introduce local land value taxes to replace council taxes and business rates. Some cities in the US (notably, Harrisburg in Pennsylvania) and elsewhere have local land value tax regimes. There are practical difficulties with implementing a land value taxation scheme in the UK in the short term – most importantly, it will require comprehensive land zoning plans and regular valuations, as well as a schedule of legitimate exemptions and reliefs. Yet, land value taxation options should be thoroughly assessed at the national and local levels of government without delay.

Revolutionising the build-for-sale market

If the essential step to address the housing crisis is to take social and affordable housing out of the hands of the finance sector and volume housebuilders, what is to be done about meeting the demand for new build housing for sale? Over decades, the housebuilders have not delivered sufficient market housing to meet this demand. As we have seen, successive government-inspired reviews and developer lobby press releases have blamed the planners for either not allocating enough land for housing, or being too slow or onerous in their requirements for planning consents. There is now, belatedly, a glimmer of light being thrown on the problems caused by the property market itself. I argue that the landowners, the volume housebuilders and their financial backers are deliberately manipulating the housing and planning system to keep up land prices. They have been amazingly successful in blaming the planners and local government, thus getting the government to intervene to help the housebuilders to build up their land banks. A review of anti-competitive practices in the housebuilding industry is long overdue.

It is time to take seriously proposals to tax land banks and implement 'use or lose it' measures. 'Use it or lose it' means that planning consents would be revoked or land compulsorily purchased if developers sit on consents for years, doing little to implement them. If a developer will not build out in time, others, including the community-led and social housing sectors, should be given the chance to build. Those threats should stop developers hoarding planning permissions and might limit land speculation. In addition, the five-year land supply measure that is widely abused by developers and landowners must be scrapped. Local authorities will be more willing to allocate land for housing if they think that it will be developed in a reliable, sustainable and community-friendly way.

To complete the picture, the Land Registry should be required to collect information on land banks and development options. To make this information more publicly accessible, local authorities should create a register of landownership for their areas so that the public can take an informed view of local authority land allocations, private and public land banks, and land purchase options.

Any measures of land reform and national housebuilding will necessitate a revolution in local government. If ever the housing crisis is to be tackled, central government must set the wheels in motion, but local authorities (in collaboration with communities) must take the lead in organising and delivering change in their local areas. Instead of the obsession with public–private partnerships, public–civic partnerships should be prioritised, bringing together public and community resources (Horvat, 2019).

Local authorities will need to be re-energised to take on this role. Property, planning, design and community development skills have been lost through cuts and restructuring. To tackle the housing crisis, local authorities must be reskilled for a civic role in housing development. For a start, local authority housing companies should accelerate building council housing. Most crucially, local councils must be given the borrowing powers (from the PWLB) and incentives to acquire land and build social housing directly, not by contracting out to the usual club of developers and consultants. Some councils have begun to build traditional high-quality council housing – a street of 105 new council homes in Norwich won the Stirling architecture prize in 2019 (Wainwright, 2019) – but this movement must be hugely expanded with government help in land and finance. Local councils must also include housing partners from the social and not-for-profit housing sectors, as well as from smaller private builders. However, this is unlikely to take place without a political revolution in local politics, which will require more far-reaching political manifestos. Slogans about building more affordable homes or council houses are not enough. Detailed plans across local authorities for a national housing drive of land acquisition, funding, the upskilling of local authority staff and direct construction, and taking on dozens of apprentices for all phases of development are needed.

The local development control process by which local authorities negotiate with housing developers needs a complete overhaul. As suggested in the case studies, the use classes order must be changed to include housing tenure classes. Viability assessment should be scrapped altogether. CIL and Section 106 need a complete rethink. If the various parts of the public and not-for-profit sectors become responsible for social and truly affordable housing as I have argued, Section 106 planning obligations should focus on other aspects of social and environmental provision. Under these circumstances, CIL should be confined to charges for hard infrastructure. To reduce speculative applications and misleading proposals, planners must be able to take into account the background and business credentials of landowners and developers as material planning considerations. 'Use it or lose it' should be in every local plan.

Scare stories

Any proposals for the radical reform of the land and planning system will provoke ferocious resistance; it would be naive to think otherwise. The *Land for the many* report from the Labour Party (2019), which contained a range of practical and well-argued land reforms, was immediately attacked by a number of national newspapers. This is a taste of things to come. If a government or local authority was elected that put forward these reforms, landowners, financiers and housebuilders would be incendiary. They will protest at the loss of land, investment opportunities and subsidy, as well as at the thought of more public scrutiny.

The Treasury will be aghast. For the property lobby, it will be the equivalent of the US health insurance industry confronted with proposals for a UK-style NHS. They will argue that the world will come crashing down, that this will be an economic disaster. The usual blockages to reform will be thrown up: the disruption to their business plans and the threat to their land banks. They will refuse to cooperate and claim that building will grind to a halt. Above all, they will claim that reforms are an attack on the very concept of private property, that they will penalise homeowners and steal their gardens.

Of course, this is untrue. Land reform and the fair taxation of land value primarily aims to provide funding and land for those in housing need. Homeowners and renters will not lose their homes or gardens. A fair system of taxation of windfall profits from land will be aimed at developers and landowners, not homeowners. Some of the most stubborn vested interests are the property professions, the RICS and the big corporate property consultants. They operate by a rule book based on market valuation practices that, as we have seen, build in ever-rising prices of land and property, and ever-decreasing land value available for local communities. This rule book must be replaced with a rule book that is about not only economic valuation, but also social and environmental valuation. There will be protests but social audits and social valuation are becoming established in other professions, so this is not impossible; it is the way ahead.[3]

Learning from the past

Reforming the land market is the biggest challenge of all. The land policy interventions of the Labour governments of the 1960s and 1970s were failures. They were unable to transfer more than a fraction of development land into public ownership, and were swiftly abolished by incoming Conservative governments. These Labour governments did not move fast enough, or have clear enough objectives. A different approach by New Labour in the 2000s of going into partnership with landowners and developers instead of trying to buy up development land also failed because of its overreliance on property market partners.

More positive lessons can be taken from the land policies of the post-war Attlee government, and from the contemporary land and planning policies of many European countries. For the first generation of new towns around London, such as Stevenage and Harlow, development land for the new towns was bought up at existing use value by new town development corporations. Instead of selling off the land to developers, it was built on directly by development corporation builders or their contractors, thus ensuring a steady supply of housing, while rents were kept to modest levels. High design standards were maintained and, crucially, land value uplift was retained by the new town corporations. Community services were provided directly alongside housing by the corporations themselves, funded, in part, by the uplift in land value.

This enlightened place-making measure was wilfully undermined by Conservative governments in the 1980s, who took the profits away from new town corporations. Instead of allowing the new towns to plough their profits from land value uplift back into their communities, the government forced the sale of new town assets and cut back on local government services that provided the lifeblood for the new towns. Although many of the new towns are now a shadow of their former ideals and intentions, the good sense of the original new town idea remains and must not be lost.

Housing land development is done far better and more equitably in other countries, particularly in mainland Europe. Some local authorities in the UK are trying to produce genuinely affordable housing and sustainable development schemes, in spite of the property lobby and government restrictions. However, there is an exceptional institutional and market resistance in the UK to adopting reform on a scale that would change the course of the housing crisis.

Above all

This book is about the finance–housebuilding complex and its hold over the housing market and the planning system. It is the major blockage to solving the UK housing crisis. Some of the aforementioned reforms on land and housebuilding will themselves help to break down the blockage, but they will not be enough. If, as I suggest, City finance and the government have become interdependent in terms of policy and the regulation of land and property, they have no interest in radical reform. Indeed, they would regard the reform of land or the housing market as dangerous for their economic model. They not only sustain the status quo, but also ensure that it is fiercely defended.

With the finance–housebuilding complex so powerful and resistant to change, what can be done? Successive Chancellors have often talked of the need to rebalance the economy away from financial services and away from London but it never happens. The London and South East property investment map dominates Treasury thinking. Rebalancing can only be taken seriously if the government acknowledges that housing is a human right and that investment means investing in people and meeting their needs, rather than investing in property values.

The government (and this means the Treasury and the Bank of England) must wean itself off economic dependency on land and house prices, with its permanent risk of boom and bust. The policy directive for the Bank of England and the Treasury must be changed from inflation control to rebalancing the economy away from the housing market, and away from London. This is not an impossible demand. There are more economically and socially beneficial – and less risky – ways of managing the economy than the current property–government embrace. If this were to happen, there will be huge social and economic benefits spreading out across the country, reversing the imbalance of the past 50 years.

None of this will happen unless ...

The housing crisis cannot to tackled and no reform is possible without political will and continued action and pressure from the grass roots – from those at the sharp end of the crisis. Research reports alone, however good, will not do it. Community-led housing and local authority initiatives across the country show that there is immense creativity and determination to do housing differently. However, governments of whatever colour will not introduce significant reforms unless they resist the property lobby. The fact is that the current fatal embrace of the government and the property lobby means that the government is no longer trusted with housing its own people. Coin Street Community Builders have a slogan: 'There is another way'. This is what is being said and demonstrated in thousands of local and national campaigns for good-quality, well-designed, genuinely affordable and environmentally sustainable housing.

We know that this is achievable at a local level and several examples have been cited in this book, and it is quite likely that this message will be better received in local authorities than in Whitehall. Local authorities who do innovate with their land, turn away from doing deals with developers, build council housing themselves, introduce their own land value capture mechanisms and work closely with local housing groups will be the pathfinders. Yet, this must be done at scale and across the whole country, and for this, the government has to step in.

Getting the government off the housing market drug – breaking its dependency on the volume housebuilders, the big landowners, investors and their City backers – is the prerequisite for tackling the housing crisis. To repeat a line from Chapter 1 of this book, planners and social housing providers at the sharp end of housing need and delivery will have no chance to deliver for their communities unless this structural imbalance is addressed.

Postscript

The property lobby was written during the political storm over Brexit and before the General Election of 2019 was called. Now that the Election has happened and Brexit is underway, a postscript is called for. What if anything will these changes mean for the property lobby?

First on Brexit. Property commentators have filled thousands of column inches debating whether Brexit will have any effect on the economy. All think it will impact the economy, but it is less clear whether EU membership as such has a specific impact on land, planning and housing that are the subject of this book. The EU does not fund housing programmes; however, new housing development in some regions often directly benefitted from EU expenditure on infrastructure, like new roads, and EU environmental regulations are an integral part of town planning law.

Will anything change in the politics of housing in the UK when we are out of EU? As the book explains, the finance-housebuilding complex has ridden out booms and slumps before, coming out more powerful after each one. Brexit will not change that. Political instability in the UK in 2016–2019 had little effect on the housing market with prices and rents continuing to rise and development being increasingly unaffordable in many parts of the country. Housebuilders profits were up; land banking continued as before; and government subsidies to the housebuilders and landowners continued. The fundamentals remained the same: a shortage of supply, high prices, and a lack of social and affordable housing, with London and the South East remaining the most attractive locations for property investors and speculators.

Some pundits predict a property boom after Brexit. They argue that pent up demand would be released, with banks and financial institutions lending more. House prices and house building rates will rise, and the housebuilders and landowners will get richer. There is evidence that soon after the 2019 election overseas investors were again buying high-end property in London (*The Guardian*, 2020). On the other hand, those opposed to leaving the EU predict an economic slow-down over the long term if there is a hard Brexit. If past history is any guide, under these circumstances, government will continue to prop up the market with Help to Buy and subsidies to the housebuilders.

The election of a Conservative government is a significant event for the property lobby (who after all partly funded the Conservative re-election campaign). Yet very little was said about housing during the General Election campaign by the Conservatives. Perhaps they think there is not a serious housing problem or that their policies from 2010 were effective in giving support to their key target homeowner and home-buyer audience. Perhaps Brexit was the only message that mattered. But does this mean that Brexit has pushed housing back down the political agenda? Or is this just a short-term reaction and in the longer-term the housing crisis will claim national attention again?

Government housing announcements over the past ten years, as this book has illustrated, are very big on rhetoric and less concerned with making a difference. The government programme set out in the Queen's Speech following the election fell into this category. It promised discounts for first time buyers and measures to strengthen tenants' rights, but there was little or nothing about building more social and affordable housing or holding down price or rent increases. More prominent was a sweeping claim to 'unleash potential of all regions across the country, leveling up every city, town and county' (MHCLG, 2019). This pledge to invest in the English regions of the North and Midlands that voted Brexit is a paradoxical one for a political party with its roots in the London and South East property market. In the final chapter of the book, refocusing the housing market away from London is a key recommendation. But are Conservatives serious about this? To turn the North and the Midlands into locations that are more attractive to property investors and developers will require long-term economic and infrastructure investment over decades to counter the attraction of London. Indeed, the finance–housebuilder complex itself might not be happy about this because this may damage their investments in the South East. On the other hand, land banking in the North may get a major boost.

Thus, it is hard to see the Conservatives changing their economic strategy in a fundamental way without offering substantial incentives to their own allies among investors, developers and landowners who have invested so much in London and South East properties over the last few decades. In addition, even if there is a major programme of infrastructure spending in the North and Midlands, there is little sign at this stage that the government understands the need for the corresponding major increases in revenue funding for local government and the public services (schools, health, social services, child care, public transport) necessary to make new (and older) communities socially and environmentally sustainable.

The absence of a Government plan to build new social and affordable housing at scale or repair the nation's housing stock is another contradiction because this is a big part of what Northern and Midland towns and cities need. Local authorities have been pushing for such measures for years, and since the general election the Local Government Association has said that a major programme of council house building is essential. 'A return to large-scale council housebuilding is the only way to boost housing supply, help families struggling to meet housing costs, provide homes to rent, reduce homelessness, and tackle the housing waiting lists many councils have' (Tanner, 2019).

Whatever happens eventually with Brexit or with the evolution of government economic policy, we can expect the main focus of government to continue on its traditional track, that is, subsidising the housebuilders, ensuring rising house prices and getting more households into the housing for sale and higher end rental markets. It is inconceivable that a new Conservative government will tackle the heart of the rigged housing and land market, for example, by taking land out of the speculative land market, or investigating the cartelisation of the housebuilding sector, both of which I argue in this book are essential. Nor is it likely that the government will address the glaring inequality in land value capture between landowners and communities that the book highlights. Government public relations may change but the property lobby will continue to dominate the shape of the UK housing and planning system for many years to come.

The reforms proposed by countless social and community housing groups for a radical land policy, a major boost to social housing, and proper regulation of property speculators, will remain as important as ever. Until a government is elected that is serious and determined to reform the housing and land markets and to build social and affordable housing at scale, community housing action and local government housing initiatives – with or without the support of central government – must be the way forward.

Notes

Chapter 1
[1] See www.coinstreet.org

Chapter 2
[1] See www.35percent.org

Chapter 3
[1] See www.smartinvestor.barclays.co.uk
[2] See www.35percent.org
[3] See www.mickbeaman.co.uk/planning
[4] See www.mickbeaman.co.uk/planning
[5] See www.mickbeaman.co.uk/planning

Chapter 4
[1] See www.mortgagestrategy.co.uk

Chapter 5
[1] See www.cla.org.uk
[2] See www.cla.org.uk
[3] See www.cla.org.uk/latest/lobbying
[4] See www.lpdf.co.uk
[5] See www.rics.org
[6] See www.generationrent.org
[7] See https://news.rla.org.uk/finance-and-tax
[8] See www.channel4.com
[9] See www.bpf.org.uk
[10] See www.bpf.org.uk
[11] See www.ukfinance.org.uk
[12] See www.35percent.org

Chapter 6
[1] See http://centaur.reading.ac.uk/71964/1/wp0317.pdf
[2] See www.localgovernmentlawyer.co.uk

Chapter 7
[1] See www.35percent.org

Chapter 8
[1] See www.labourland.org
[2] See www.communitylandtrusts.org.uk

Chapter 9

[1] See www.35percent.org
[2] See www.awics.co.uk
[3] See www.realassets.ipe.com
[4] See www.lada.debtresistance.uk

Chapter 10

[1] See www.oxford.gov.uk
[2] See www.oxfordnorth.com/about

Chapter 11

[1] See www.westminster.ac.uk/research/groups-and-centres/highbury-group-on-housing-delivery
[2] See www.labourland.org
[3] See www.socialauditnetwork.org.uk

References

Adams, D. (1984) *Urban planning and the development process*, London: Routledge.

Adams, D. and Leishman, C. (2008) 'Factors affecting build out rates' [policy research paper], Department of Urban Studies, University of Glasgow.

Adams, G. (2018) Mortgage Strategy, 5 September.

Albeers, M. (2016) *The financialisation of housing: A political economy approach*, London: Routledge.

Ambrose, P. and Colenutt, B. (1975) *The property machine*, London: Penguin Books.

Apps, P. (2019) 'Twenty flats destroyed in huge Barking flat fire', *Inside Housing,* 10 September.

Aubrey, T. (2018) *How changing land law can unlock England's housing potential*, London: Centre for Progressive Policy.

Ball, M. (1983) *Housing policy and economic power*, New York, NY: Methuen.

Barker, K. (2004) *Review of housing supply*, London: HMSO.

Barras, R. (2009) *Building cycles: growth and instability*, Oxford: Wiley-Blackwell.

Barratt, L. (2018a) 'Scrapping the borrowing cap will deliver only 9000 additional homes', *Inside Housing*, 29 October.

Barratt, L. (2018b) 'First Priority: the inside story of a housing association that almost went bust', *Inside Housing*, 9 November.

Baum, A. (2015) *Real estate investment* (3rd edn), London: Routledge.

Baynes, C. (2019) 'Property giants pay £63m which escalates the housing crisis by sitting on enough land for 470,000 homes', *The Independent*, 6 September.

BBC (2018) 'Haringey council row: authority scraps £2bn housing project', *BBC News*, 19 September.

Bentley, D. (2017) *The land question*, London: Civitas.

Beswick, J. and Penny, J. (2018) 'Demolishing the present to sell off the future: the emergence of "financialised municipal entrepreneurialism" in London', *International Journal of Urban and Regional Research*, 42(2) May, https://doi.org/10.1111/1468-2427.12612 [Accessed 18 November 2019].

Blake, H. (2011) 'Conservatives given millions by property developers', *Daily Telegraph*, 9 September.

Booth, R. (2017) 'Foreign investors snapping up London homes suitable for first-time buyers', *The Guardian*, 13 June.

Booth, R. (2018) 'Tory Westminster councillor resigns after hospitality inquiry', *The Guardian*, 10 October.

Booth, R. and Crossley, F. (2018) 'Nearly 100 London councillors have links to property industry', *The Guardian*, 29 April.

Bowie, D. (2017) *Radical solutions to the housing supply crisis*, London: Routledge.

BPF (British Property Federation) (2013) *Investing in residential property*, London: BPF.

Brownill, S. and Bradley, Q. (2017) *Localism and neighbourhood planning*, Bristol: Policy Press.

Brownill, S., Cho, Y., Karvani, R., Nase, I., Downing, L., Valler, D., Whitehouse, N. and Bernstock, P. (2015) *Rethinking planning obligations: balancing housing numbers and affordability*, York: Joseph Rowntree Foundation.

Cahill, K. (2001) *Who owns Britain?*, Edinburgh: Canongate.

Callcutt, J. (2007) *Review of housebuilding delivery*, London: HMSO.

Centre for Progressive Policy (2018) 'Landowners make £13bn profit in one year', September, www.progressive-policy.net/press-releases/press-release-landowners-make-13bn-profit-in-one-year-as-high-land-prices-stifle-affordable-housing [Accessed 17 December 2019].

Chakrabortty, A. (2014) 'The truth about gentrification: regeneration or con-trick', *The Guardian*, 18 May.

Champ, H. (2018), 'Extend Help to Buy or face house building disaster, warns CPA', *Building*, 5 October.

Chapman, B. (2018) 'Competition watchdog sends tough message to business cheats with cartel campaign', *The Independent*, 22 October.

Christophers, B. (2018) *The new enclosure*, London: Verso.

CIH (Chartered Institute for Housing) (2018) *UK housing review*, London: CIH.

CLA (Country Landowners Association) (2013) 'Response to community infrastructure levy' [press release], April.

CLA (2018a) 'Response to developer contributions', submission to House of Commons Committee on Land Value, 10 May.

CLA (2018b) 'Land value capture wrong way to solve the housing crisis' [press release] 13 September.

CLA (2018c) 'Statement on Labour Party planning review' [press release], 24 September.

Clancy, R. (2018) 'Landlords told they have an important role in building new homes in England', *Property Wire*, 20 November.

Clarence-Smith, L., Ellson, A. and Wright, O. (2019) 'Persimmon faces loss of Help to Buy homes contract', *The Times*, 23 February.

Clover, C. (2017) 'A history of the CLA (Country Landowners Association)', *Three Acres and a Cow*, https://threeacresandacow.co.uk/2017/08/a-history-of-the-cla-the-country-landowners-association [Accessed 18 November 2019].

Cochrane, A., Colenutt, B. and Field, M. (2015) 'Governing the ungovernable: spatial politics, market housing and volume housebuilders', *Policy & Politics*, 43(4): 527–44.

Coleman, A. (1985) *Utopia on trial*, London: Hilary Shipman.

Collinson, P. (2017) 'Four in ten Right to Buy homes now owned by private landlords', *The Guardian*, 8 December.

Collison, P. (1963) *Cutteslowe walls: A study in social class*, London: Faber & Faber.

Colville, R. (2019) 'Time to stop punishing London's landlords', *Evening Standard*, 11 February.

Conservative Party (2010) *Open source planning*, London: Conservative Party.

Copley, T. (2019) *Right to Buy: Wrong for London*, London: London Labour.

CPRE (Campaign to Protect Rural England) (2018) *State of the Green Belt 2018*, London: CPRE.

Crane, H. (2017) 'EcoWorld buys majority stake in Willmott Dixon's Be Living', *Property Week*, 8 November.

Crisis (2018) *How to end homelessness in Britain*, London: Crisis.

Crosby, N., Daveney, S. and Wyatt, P. (2017) 'The implied internal rate of return in conventional residual valuations of development sites', Working Paper on Real Estate and Planning 03/17, University of Reading.

Cullingworth, B. (1999) *British planning: 50 years of urban and regional policy*, London: Athlone Press.

Da Silva, M. (2019) 'UK rents rise 13 per cent in last five years', *Landlord Today*, 11 July.

DCLG (Department for Communities and Local Government) (2012) *National Planning Policy Framework*, London: DCLG.

Dominiczak, P. (2015) 'George Osborne to force councils to build homes in overhaul of the planning system', *Daily Telegraph*, 9 July.

Doward, J. (2018) 'Housing crisis drives more than 1m private tenants deeper into poverty', *The Guardian*, 22 September.

Dransfield, L. (2018) 'Grosvenor readies strategic land drive', *Radius Data Exchange*, 29 November.

Edwards, M. (2015) *Prospects for land, rent and housing in UK cities*, Foresight Report, Government Office for Science.

Elliott, L. (2018) 'At last a reason to celebrate: house prices are falling', *The Guardian*, 10 May.

Ellis, H. and Henderson, K. (2016) *English planning in crisis*, Bristol: Policy Press.

Evening Standard (2018) 'First time buyers' [supplement], *Evening Standard*, 26 July.

Falk, N. (2019) 'Sharing the uplift in land values: a fairer system for funding and delivering housing growth', *Town and Country Planning*, 88(8): 2–48.

Farlow, A. (2013) *The crash and beyond*, Oxford: Oxford University Press.

Field, M. (2020) *Creating community-led and self-build homes*, Bristol: Policy Press.

Garber, S. (2018) 'Shrinking homes: the average British house 20 per cent smaller than in the 1970s', *Which?* 14 April.

Gerrity, M. (2019) 'Brexit uncertainty continues to impact London's luxury housing market', *World Property Journal*, 27 August.

GOV.UK (2019) *Viability Guidance*, Ministry of Housing, Communities and Local Government, September.

Grant, H. and Mohdin, A. (2019) '"Outrageous and disgusting": segregated playground sparks fury', *The Guardian*, 29 March.

Grayston, R. (2017) *Slipping through the loophole*, London: Shelter.

Greenwood, X. and Adams, R. (2018) 'Oxford and Cambridge university colleges own property worth £3.5bn', *The Guardian*, 29 May.

Gregory, A. (2018) 'Jeremy Hunt avoids £100,000 stamp duty by exploiting Tory tax loophole by buying flats in the UK', *Daily Mirror*, 23 April.

The Guardian (2018) 'The UK's house price boom is slowing: and that's welcome news', *The Guardian*, 30 December.

The Guardian (2020) 'So far the Tories' promises to tackle the housing crisis have proved to be empty', *The Guardian*, 6 January.

Gulliver, K. (2017) 'Britain's housing crisis is racist – we need to talk about it', *The Guardian*, 6 July.

Hall, P. (1973) *The containment of urban England*, London: Allen & Unwin.

Harman, J. (2012) *Viability testing local plans*, London: NHBC (National House Building Council) and the Local Government Association.

Harrison, M., Phillipps, D., Chahal, K., Hunt, L. and Perry, J. (2005) *Housing race and community cohesion*, London: Chartered Institute for Housing.

Heywood, A. (2012), *London for sale?*, London: Smith Institute.

HM Treasury (2011) *Plan or growth*, London: HM Treasury.

Holly, N. (2018) 'Lessons for planning and development from a pioneer of locally led growth, *Town and Country Planning*, 87(12): 509–14.

Horvat, V. (2018) *Real Democracy in your town; public-civic partnerships in action*, Brussels: Green European Foundation.

House of Commons Public Accounts Committee (2019) 'Planning and the broken housing market', HC 1744.

Housebuilder (2017) 'Britain's biggest housebuilders', *Housebuilder*, October.

Housebuilder (2018) 'Britain's biggest housebuilders', *Housebuilder*, October: 27–44.

Inman, P. (2018), 'UK's wealth rises as land values soar by $450bn in a year', *The Guardian*, 29 August.

Isaac, D. and O'Leary, J. (2011) *Property investment*, London: Palgrave Macmillan.

ITV (2018) 'Britain's property crisis', *Tonight*, 27 September.

Jacobs, J. (1961) *The life and death of great American cities*, London: Vintage.

Jenkins, S. (2018) 'Luxury towers wreck cities – yet Britain still builds them', *The Guardian*, 29 May.

Johnson, P. (2019) 'Doubling of the housing benefit bill is sign of something deeply wrong', *The Times*, 4 March.

Jones, A. (2019) 'The housing associations building luxury flats over social homes', *Vice News*, 20 August.

Jones, O. (2014) *The establishment*, London: Allen Lane.

Kentish, B. (2018) 'Buy to Let landlords stop 2.2 million families becoming homeowners, report by Tory MP finds', *Independent*, 23 June.

King, P. (2006) *Choice and the end of social housing*, London: IEA (Institute of Economic Affairs).

King, P. (2010) *Housing policy transformed: the Right to Buy and the desire to own*, Bristol: Policy Press.

Kitson, R. (2014) 'Bitter row over £5bn Greenwich housing plan branded "social cleansing" by critics', *Evening Standard*, 23 September.

Klein, N. (2014) *This changes everything*, London: Penguin.

Knight Frank (2018) *Survey of barriers to housing*, London: Knight Frank.

Kollewe, J. (2014) 'London retains crown as favourite city of the ultra-rich', *The Guardian*, 5 March.

Labour Party (2019) *Land for the many*, London: Labour Party.

Landlord Today (2018) 'Over 65s have gained £5.5bn of property wealth over past 12 months', *Landlord Today*, 29 August, www.landlordtoday. co.uk/breaking-news/2019/6/over-65s-have-gained-5-5bn-of-property-wealth-over-past-12-months [Accessed 19 December 2019].

Lane, M. (2019) 'London revealed as one of Europe's major Build to Rent hotspots', *Property Investor Today*, 31 July.

Leishman, C. and Warren, F. (2005) 'Planning for consumer new-build housing choices', in D. Adams, C. Watkins and M. White (eds) *Planning, public policy and property markets*, Oxford: Blackwell, pp 167–84.

Letwin, O. (2018) *Independent review of build out: final report*, CM 9720, London: MHCLG and HM Treasury.

Lichfield Consultants (2018) *Realising potential: the scale and role of specialist land promotion in housing delivery*, London: Lichfield Consultants.

Lizieri, C., Reinart, J. and Baum, A. (2011) *Who owns the city 2011: change and global ownership of City of London offices*, Real Estate Finance Group, University of Cambridge.

LGA (Local Government Association) (2013) *Probity in planning*, London: Local Government Association.

Massey, M. and Catalano, A. (1978) *Capital and land*, London: Arnold.

Mathiason, N., Newman, M. and McClenghan, M. (2012) *Revealed: The £93m City lobby machine*, London: Bureau of Investigative Journalists.

MHCLG (Ministry of Housing, Communities and Local Government) (2018) *Revised National Planning Policy Framework*, London: MHCLG.

MHCLG (2019a) *National Planning Policy Framework*, London: MHCLG.

MHCLG (2019b) 'House building; new build dwellings, England: September Quarter 2018'. Housing Statistical Release, 15 January, London: MHCLG.

MHCLG (2019c) 'Queen's speech: delivering fairer, more affordable homes for buyers and renters' [press release], 19 December.

Minton, A. (2017) *Big capital: Who is London for?* London: Penguin Books.

Monbiot, G. (2012) 'Richard Benyon: the minister destroying what he is paid to protect', *The Guardian*, 20 April.

Monk, S., Lister, D., Short, C., Whitehead, C.M.E., Crook, A.D.H. and Rowley, S. (2005) *Land and finance for affordable housing*, York: Joseph Rowntree Foundation.

Moore, V. (1987) *A practical approach to planning law*, Oxford: Oxford University Press.

Morphet, J. (2017) *Local authority direct provision of housing*, London: RTPI (Royal Town Planning Institute).

Myers, R. (2017) 'Philip Hammond could make millions on green belt land he owns next to his house', *Daily Mirror*, 9 July.

National Housing Federation (2018) *Landowners make £13bn profit in one year as high land prices stifle affordable housing*, London: National Housing Federation.

Neale, R. (2019) 'Outrage as help-to-buy boosts Persimmon profits to £1bn', *The Guardian*, 26 February.

Neale, R., Mathiason, N. and Turner, G. (2018) 'Berkeley calls affordable housing targets "unviable" as chairman earns £174m', *The Guardian*, 3 September.

Nolan, L. (1997) *Report of the Committee on Standards in Public Life*, London: HMSO.

Norton-Taylor, R. (1982) *Whose land is it anyway?*, London: Twinstone Press.

OFT (Office of Fair Trading) (2008) *Homebuilding in the UK: a market study*, London: OFT.

Open University (2017) *Tensions and prospects: research project*, www.open.ac.uk [Accessed 19 December 2019].

Payne, S. (2015) 'Exploring the impact of the recession on British volume housebuilders', *Built Environment*, 42(2): 271–88.

PEACH (People's Empowerment Alliance for Custom House) (2018) *People's Empowerment Plan for Custom House*, London: PEACH.

Phillips, M. (2017) 'UK property market famous names are bankrolling the 2017 General Election', Bisnow, 6 June.

Pidd, H, (2018) 'London falling: how the North of England got its groove back', *The Guardian*, 18 May.

Portlock, R. (2018) *UK residential property: institutional attitudes*, Investment International Property Forum Research.

(RLA) Residential Landlords Association (2018) 'Landlords could be offered financial incentives for longer tenancies', https://news.rla.org.uk/landlords-financial-incentives/ [Accessed 18 November 2019].

Resolution Foundation (2018) *Home improvements: action to address the housing challenges faced by young people*, London: Resolution Foundation.

Rex, J. and Moore, R. (1967) *Race, community and conflict: a study of Sparkbrook*, Oxford: Oxford University Press.

RICS (Royal Institution of Chartered Surveyors) (2017) *RICS valuation – global standards 2017*, London: RICS.

Robinson, J. and Attuyer, K. (2019) 'Old Oak Common' [unpublished paper] University College London.

Rowntree, J. (2016) 'Disproportionate presence of Conservative Party donors and supporters', www.property118.com/92625-2 [Accessed 18 November 2019].

Ryan-Collins, J., Lloyd, T. and McFarlane, L. (2017) *Rethinking the economics of land and housing*, London: Zed Books.

Rydin, Y. (1993) *The British planning system: an introduction*, London: Macmillan.

Rydin, Y. (2013) *The future of planning*, Bristol: Policy Press.

Sassen, S. (2014) *Expulsions*, Cambridge, MA: Harvard University Press.

Sassen, S. (2015) 'Who owns our cities – and why this urban takeover should concern us all', *The Guardian*, 24 November.

Savills (2018) 'How do we reach 300,000 homes? And who will build them? *Savills*, 15 October, www.savills.co.uk/research_articles/229130/267515-0/how-do-we-reach-300-000-homes--and-who-will-build-them [Accessed 18 November 2019].

Shelter (2018) *A vision for social housing*, London: Shelter.

Short, J.R., Fleming, S. and Witt, S. (1986) *Housebuilding and community action*, London: Routledge.

Shrubsole, G. (2019) *Who owns England?* London: William Collins.

Slade, D. (2018) 'The reform of planning practice, and the practice of planning reform: how "everyday" national-level policymaking practices shape planning and spatial governance' [PhD thesis] University of Liverpool.

Sommerlad, N. (2019) 'Boris Johnson's campaign funded by billionaires behind £100m development he approved', *Daily Mirror*, 4 July.

Spencer, B. and Taylor, R. (2014) 'Developers ruining our countryside: they bankroll farmers seeking permission to build in their fields', *Daily Mail*, 23 November.

Sylvester, R. (2018) 'Greedy housebuilders face losing Right to Build', *The Times*, 31 January.

Tanner, B. (2019) 'LGA tells government to prioritise council housebuilding', *24 Housing*, 19 December, www.24housing.co.uk/news/lga-tells-government-to-prioritise-council-housebuilding/ [Accessed 20 December 2019].

TCPA (Town and Country Planning Association) (2018a) '98% of councils say new development does not meet affordable housing policy' [press release], 8 May, London: TCPA.

TCPA (2018b) *The Raynsford review of planning*, London: TCPA.

Varoufakis, Y. (2017) *Adults in the room*, London: Vintage.

Wainwright, O. (2019) 'A masterpiece: Norwich Council houses win Stirling Architecture Prize', *The Guardian*, 8 October.

Wates, N. (1976) *The battle for Tolmers Square*, London: Routledge.

Watt, P. (forthcoming) *Estate regeneration and its disasters: Public housing, place and inequality in London*, Bristol: Policy Press.

Wellings, F. (2006) *British housebuilders*, Oxford: Blackwell.

Wheatley, H. (2019) *Mass sell-off of public land is driving the housing crisis*, London: New Economics Foundation.

White, C. (2017) 'Every flat in new London estate has been sold to foreign investors', *Metro*, 16 April.

Wightman, A. (1996) *Who owns Scotland?*, Edinburgh: Canongate.

Young, C. and Balch, C. (2010) 'Affordability, viability and planning gain – will it deliver?', Midlands Planning and Policy Conference.

Index

W

waiting lists 1, 121–2, 131, 135
Wales 102
Wellings, F. 27
West Northants Development
    Corporation (WNDC) 88
Westbury Homes 28
Westminster City Council Planning
    Committee 77
Whittaker, Andrew 91
Wightman, A. 49, 149

Wikipedia 78
Wilcon Homes 28
Willmott Dixon 30
windfalls 47, 68
    and affordable housing 107, 108
    and land value 60–2, 110–11, 155
Woodberry Down, Hackney 22, 121–2
workers, key 11, 23, 126

Y

young people 3, 23

Printed in Great Britain
by Amazon